What Comes After Faith?

Kenneth Hagin Jr.

Unless otherwise indicated, all Scripture quotations in this volume are from the *King James Version* of the Bible.

First Edition
Second Printing 1993

ISBN 0-89276-727-8

In the U.S. write:
Kenneth Hagin Ministries
P.O. Box 50126
Tulsa, OK 74150-0126

In Canada write:
Kenneth Hagin Ministries
P.O. Box 335
Islington (Toronto), Ontario
Canada, M9A 4X3

He Gave Gifts Unto Men:
 A Biblical Perspective of Apostles, Prophets, and Pastors
 The Price Is Not Greater Than God's Grace (Mrs. Oretha Hagin)

MINIBOOKS (A partial listing)

* *The New Birth
* *Why Tongues?
* *In Him
* *God's Medicine
* *You Can Have What You Say
  *How To Write Your Own Ticket With God
* *Don't Blame God
* *Words
  *Plead Your Case
* *How To Keep Your Healing
  *The Bible Way To Receive the Holy Spirit
  *I Went to Hell
  *How To Walk in Love
  *The Precious Blood of Jesus
* *Love Never Fails
  *Learning To Flow With the Spirit of God
  *The Glory of God
  *Hear and Be Healed
  *Knowing What Belongs to Us
  *Your Faith in God Will Work

BOOKS BY KENNETH HAGIN JR.

* *Man's Impossibility — God's Possibility
  *Because of Jesus
  *How To Make the Dream God Gave You Come True
  *The Life of Obedience
  *God's Irresistible Word
  *Healing: Forever Settled
  *Don't Quit! Your Faith Will See You Through
  *The Untapped Power in Praise
  *Listen to Your Heart
  *What Comes After Faith?

MINIBOOKS (A partial listing)

* *Faith Worketh by Love
  *Blueprint for Building Strong Faith
* *Seven Hindrances to Healing
* *The Past Tense of God's Word
  *Faith Takes Back What the Devil's Stolen
  *"The Prison Door Is Open — What Are You Still Doing Inside?"
  *How To Be a Success in Life
  *Get Acquainted With God
  *Showdown With the Devil
  *Unforgiveness
  *Ministering to the Brokenhearted

*These titles are also available in Spanish. Information about other foreign translations of several of the above titles (i.e., Finnish, French, German, Indonesian, Polish, Russian, Norwegian, Portuguese, Korean, Japanese, Chinese Mandarin, etc.) may be obtained by writing to: Kenneth Hagin Ministries, P.O. Box 50126, Tulsa, Oklahoma 74150-0126.

Contents

Chapter 1
And Beside This

Throughout the church world today, there seems to be a universal problem. Somewhere along the line, the spiritual growth of most Christians has become stunted. Sad to say, there are countless numbers of believers who are living weak, defeated, anemic lives. Why is this? More importantly, is there an answer to this problem? If there is, we need to know it. I believe the apostle Peter gives us the solution in 2 Peter 1:1-11:

2 PETER 1:1-11
1   Simon Peter, a servant and an apostle of Jesus Christ, to them that have obtained like precious faith with us through the righteousness of God and our Saviour Jesus Christ:
2   Grace and peace be multiplied unto you through the knowledge of God, and of Jesus our Lord,
3   According as his divine power hath given unto us all things that pertain unto life and godliness, through the knowledge of him that hath called us to glory and virtue:
4   Whereby are given unto us exceeding great and precious promises: that by these ye might be partakers of the divine nature, having escaped the corruption that is in the world through lust.
5   And beside this, giving all diligence, add to your faith virtue; and to virtue knowledge;
6   And to knowledge temperance; and to temperance patience; and to patience godliness;
7   And to godliness brotherly kindness; and to

brotherly kindness charity.
8   For if these things be in you, and abound, they
make you that ye shall neither be barren nor
unfruitful in the knowledge of our Lord Jesus
Christ.
9   But he that lacketh these things is blind, and
cannot see afar off, and hath forgotten that he was
purged from his old sins.
10 Wherefore the rather, brethren, give diligence
to make your calling and election sure: for if ye do
these things, ye shall never fall:
11 For so an entrance shall be ministered unto
you abundantly into the everlasting kingdom of
our Lord and Saviour Jesus Christ.

Putting Them in Remembrance

Before we look at these verses in detail, let's con-
sider the background in which Peter wrote them. It was
somewhere around AD 66. Peter knew he was facing
martyrdom soon. He says, *"Knowing that shortly I must*
put off this my tabernacle, even as our Lord Jesus
Christ hath shewed me. Moreover I will endeavour that
ye may be able after my decease to have these things
always in remembrance" (2 Peter 1:14,15).

Even though he knew death was before him, Peter
was not negative or depressed. He was very positive
and joyful in writing to the Church. However, he was
also very concerned about them. A lot of carnality had
evidently crept into the lives of the believers. And the
Church at that time was under attack from all kinds of
crazy doctrines from false teachers. Sounds a lot like
the Church today, doesn't it?

The believers then were dwelling on minor issues that didn't amount to a whole lot. They had digressed from the main point of the gospel of Jesus Christ. Some were being led into heresy. In this epistle, Peter is trying to pull them back into line. He's reminding them and exhorting them what to do to stand strong in faith and be fruitful.

Notice right from the start, Peter is talking to believers. He makes this clear by saying, ". . . *to them that have obtained like precious faith with us . . ."* (2 Peter 1:1). Every believer has been given the measure of faith (Rom. 12:3). The Bible tells us many things that we are to do with that measure of faith. We are to walk by faith and not by sight (2 Cor. 5:7). We're to fight the good fight of faith (1 Tim. 6:12). It also says that without faith it is impossible to please God (Heb. 11:6). As you can see, the Bible has a lot to say about faith.

Lots of people walk around declaring, "I'm a faith person." "I'm this," and "I'm that," but their lives are a mess. Yes, we are to be people of faith. That does not mean people of foolishness, presumption, or stupidity. There have been many things done in the name of faith that have nothing to do with faith whatsoever. If we'd all just use a little more common sense, mistakes wouldn't be made that bring a reproach to the gospel.

Abundance of Grace and Peace

Peter goes on to say, *"Grace and peace be multiplied*

unto you through the knowledge of God, and of Jesus our Lord" (2 Peter 1:2). I like this verse because it tells us that our God is the God of abundance. He is El Shaddai. He wants us to have more than just a little bit of grace and peace, more than just enough to barely get by. He wants to give us *multiplied* grace and peace. That means grace and peace in abundance. In these last days, we will need more grace and peace than we have ever needed before to walk by faith.

God does indeed give us everything we need. In the next couple of verses it says that we've been given all things that pertain to life and godliness and all the promises so that we can participate in His divine nature (2 Peter 1:3,4). Right here, is where a lot of Christians miss it.

Most Christians read verses 3 and 4 and they go around with big smiles on their faces proudly and boldly confessing, "I'm a partaker of His divine nature. I've been given all things that pertain to life and godliness." All that is true, true, true! But verses 3 and 4 don't end there. There's more to it than that.

Peter goes on to write, *"And beside this . . ."* (2 Peter 1:5). In other words, he was saying, "That's not all there is; there's something else besides being a partaker of His divine nature; there's something else besides having all the promises; there's something else."

That's what it means, *"And beside this."* Haven't you ever noticed that when you are talking to someone, you'll usually leave the best till last. If there's something you particularly want to emphasize, you'll say,

"And besides this, do such and such." In other words, you're saying, "Do everything else I just told you, but make sure you don't forget to do this last thing."

That's exactly what Peter did. He just got everybody excited talking about being a partaker of God's divine nature, telling the people they could have everything needed for life and godliness. It's almost like he softened them up with the "life and godliness words" but now he's ready to hit them with what he really wants them to get. The heavy stuff's coming up next.

The bottom line of what he really wanted to say to them was this: You have to grow up spiritually. It's time to go on. The blessings are great; you need them to live victoriously here on earth but now, let's grow up and add something else to it. You need something else in your life — it's called Christian character.

Goosebump Christianity

When you say, "Let's develop Christian character," everybody groans. Everybody likes the goosebump part of Christianity — the part that get us all excited — but when it comes to the nitty, gritty parts of Christianity, then people want to go hide in a cave. That's foolish. It's vitally necessary that we mature spiritually — then and only then will we ever really enjoy the blessings that God has for us.

That's what these verses in Second Peter chapter 1 are all about — growing up spiritually — becoming God's person of strong Christian character. Is that ever needed in the Church today! As a whole, the Church is sorely lacking in overall Christian character. As a result, people just go and do whatever they want to do and it gives a bad name to Christianity.

If we would grow up spiritually and I'm talking about intelligent spirituality, we would be people of integrity — people of godliness and virtue. The world would then look at us and see a big difference between us and them and wonder why. There should be a *big* difference between us and them. That difference comes in Christian character.

You see everyone loves to confess for the big houses and the boat by the lake and the fancy clothes and so on. What good does that do anybody if they are so spiritually immature? They continue to walk just like the rest of the world. It's time we grew up. We should be different and it should show.

Besides being partakers of His divine nature, enjoying all the blessings and promises, there is more we are to have in our Christian walk. What exactly is it that Peter wants us to add to our lives to make us different, to make us spiritually mature?

Peter desired that the Church walk strong in faith. You can't do that without strong Christian character. Let's look at what else Peter tells us to do with our faith besides just enjoying all the blessings.

Peter says to *give all diligence* to adding certain things to our faith. Right there is where we lose a lot of people. Mention the promises and everybody gets all excited. But mention a word like diligence and forget it.

Nobody likes that little word "diligence" because it implies something. Diligence means W-O-R-K. Giving all diligence to something means that you work at it. Diligence is characterized by perseverance — giving a steady, earnest, energetic application to something. When you give diligence to something, you prove you esteem it.

Most Christians balk at that idea. They want things to just fall out of Heaven on their heads. Peter knew this. That's why he wrote these verses. He was saying to the believers, "Listen up folks! There is something you have to do."

What is it we have to do? Giving all diligence, we're to add to our faith some things, some very important things. You may be saying, "Now wait a minute. I thought we all had the same measure of faith. How can we add to it?"

Yes, we do all have the same measure of faith. We got that when we were born again. But we can add to it. If we couldn't, Peter would never have said we could. Adding to our faith simply means making our faith better, improving it, enhancing it, and making it stronger. If there's something I can do to improve my faith and make it stronger, I want to know what it is, don't you?

Chapter 2

Adding Virtue: Power Within

What exactly was it that Peter said to add to our faith, with all diligence? Actually, he said there's several things we need to add. The first thing is *virtue*. Without virtue being added, our faith can be very shallow.

The word *virtue* has many different meanings. It can mean "morality," "excellence," "valor," or "strength." It can also mean "power." That's the definition I like best.

We see the word virtue used as power in the story about the sick woman with the issue of blood. She'd been sick for many years and had gone to several doctors to no avail. Then she heard Jesus was in town.

MARK 5:27-30
27 When she had heard of Jesus, [she] came in the press behind, and touched his garment.
28 For she said, If I may touch but his clothes, I shall be whole.
29 And straightway the fountain of her blood was dried up; and she felt in her body that she was healed of that plague.
30 And Jesus, immediately knowing in himself that virtue had gone out of him, turned him about in the press, and said, Who touched my clothes?

It says that the moment this sick woman touched

Jesus, He knew that virtue had gone out of Him. And He said, "Who touched me?" I'm sure as soon as He uttered those words, the disciples looked at Him like He was nuts. There were hundreds of people all crowding around Him; any one of several could have touched Him.

But you see, that woman touched Him in a different way than all the rest, and He knew it. She touched him with faith, believing for her miracle. When she did, virtue was released from Jesus. What was that virtue? It was power. Power was released from Him and that's how He knew He'd been touched. He felt that power go out from Him.

Christian Energy in You

In Second Peter 1:5, *The Amplified Bible* calls this virtue, "excellence, resolution, and Christian energy"! If there's one thing Christians need today, it's energy! Christian energy will rid your life of laziness! Energy doesn't just sit still. Energy produces something. Energy gets you up and keeps you going.

We've got too many Christians today who are just sitting around, not doing much of anything. That's why the world is in the mess it's in. That's why your community or state is in the mess it's in, and that's why your family and neighbors are a mess. We've nobody to blame but ourselves because for the most part, we've just sat around patting ourselves on the back saying, "Glory, hallelujah. I'm so glad Jesus set me free."

Jesus set us free for a reason. And it's not to just sit around. If you add energy — virtue — power — to your faith, you will get out there and help set others free. It's not enough just for your life to be running over with all the blessings. You need to get up and see that others enjoy them, too. We've been blessed to be a blessing, not to just sit and do nothing.

No Retirement Plan

Some Christians I know remind me of the "old stick whittlers" of Texas. In some of those old Texan towns, there's a square right in the middle of town. It's usually right in front of the courthouse with a fountain somewhere around and a bunch of benches. This is before the days of the super-malls, obviously!

All these little businesses around the square had benches sitting out in front of them and people would just sit down and talk and whittle the day away. A lot of those old men got to be real good whittlers, too, because they had nothing else to do but sit around, talk and whittle. Most of them were now enjoying their retirement, and they'd just sit there and watch their kids and grandkids hustling and bustling all over town. Not them, though. Their idea of Heaven was sitting and doing absolutely nothing but talk and whittle.

That's fine for them; they deserve to enjoy their retirement. But it's not fine for Christians today. In the Christian world, there is never room for retirement. We just refire! We need to get up, get moving, and extend some of that energy, that virtue, that's in us. Add virtue to your faith and your faith will be powerful.

James says your faith without works is *dead*.

JAMES 2:17
17 Even so faith, if it hath not works, is dead, being alone.

It's not enough to sit around making faith confessions without doing anything. It won't work. Your faith has to have some kind of corresponding action to it or it is worthless. If you'll add virtue to your faith, your faith will have all the energy it needs to act.

Roller-Coaster Christianity

We have too many roller-coaster Christians around; we don't need any more. Do you know what I mean by a roller-coaster Christian? It means one who is up one day, down the next, up and down continually. It's those people who are so high on Jesus during a church service that they about bang their heads on the top of the door walking out. But as soon as they leave the meeting, they're down again until the next one. That's just immature. They will never grow that way.

They're the people who always seem to be getting beat up. As soon as they leave the church, they start going downhill fast. This is what I call *excited faith*. They can be all excited while in the church service but the second they leave and the devil hits them with something, they're done for. *Excited faith* that is up one day and down the next won't do a whole lot for God. The faith that gets something done is faith that has virtue, power, energy added to it. It's a mature, strong faith. It's a faith based on the facts of God's Word, not circumstances or emotions.

You see, excited faith never fully matures. It stays weak and anemic. You know, we've been thrown so much spiritual candy, we're almost diabetic spiritually. Our faith needs to grow up. It needs to be energized and strengthened. Virtue will do that.

Have you ever tried to push a car out of mud? In north central Texas, they have this mud that's called "old black gumbo." When it gets really wet, you'll just keep sinking into that mud until you're knee-deep and then you're stuck.

When you're knee-deep in mud yourself, you can't help anyone else. You can't push a car out of it because it takes all the energy you've got to just lift your own legs, much less lift anything else.

That's exactly what is happening in the Christian world today. People are knee-deep in muck and mire and they're trying to pull themselves out but it's taking all the energy they've got just to move their own feet, much less take on the devil and his cohorts or help anyone else.

Fortifying the Inner Man

Many Christians go along and as long as everything's nice and smooth they're happy. But the second a trial or temptation comes, they're done in. That should not be. We must keep our energy level up. It's vitally necessary that we add virtue to our faith. Just because you learn how to believe God and know how to make 18,000 faith confessions, does not mean that you will mature spiritually. A lot of people think just because they can believe God for a bunch of stuff that they are spiritually mature. That's not necessarily so. You can have faith — because everyone who is born again has a measure of faith — and still be a spiritual baby.

It's what we add to that original measure of faith that really counts. There's a lot of carnal Christians running around who haven't added much of anything to their faith. Then when the going gets rough, they're the ones who scream the loudest! They come running to you whining, "Oh, Brother Hagin, I just don't know whether I'm going to make it or not! I just feel so weak, I'm just so down."

Their spiritual man needs to be fortified. We see the commercials about new fortified cereals and extra strength vitamins. We need that for our spiritual man just as much as our natural, physical body needs it. Energy — virtue — is what will keep you fortified, and keep you strong. It develops strength in you so when the enemy comes in, you can rise up strong and fight him off without getting all down and weak.

No Christian should be down and weak. We have all the power we need to be up and strong.

ROMANS 8:11
11 But if the Spirit of him that raised up Jesus

from the dead dwell in you, he that raised up Christ from the dead shall also quicken your mortal bodies by his Spirit that dwelleth in you.

You have a powerhouse living on the inside of you — He's called the Holy Spirit. He will quicken or energize your mortal body! When a person's energy level is low, he's more easily tempted than when he is running at a high energy level. Maintain a high level of energy by fortifying your inner man and you won't have as much trouble with temptation.

Climb Out of that Spiritual Cradle

Peter told us to add virtue to your faith. To *add* means you have to do something. People say, "But I just want to sit back and float through life on flowery beds of ease." People who think like that will remain in the same spiritual cradle they were born in unless they get up and begin to add something to their faith.

Have you ever noticed that some people attain a certain chronological age, but their emotional and mental age is far less? They're thirty-five years old on the outside, but they act like they're still twenty-five or fifteen! They simply need to grow up.

We have the same thing happening in the spiritual world. We have fifteen-, twenty-, and thirty-year-old Christians (chronologically) who are acting like two-year-olds. When they are faced with some of the problems and challenges life throws at them, they can't handle it. They haven't grown up at all. Why? Because they're lazy! That's right. Let's face it, human beings as a whole are basically lazy creatures! We always want somebody else to do it for us.

Our Heavenly Father expects us to grow up. Wouldn't I look silly trying to carry around my son, Craig, who is in his twenties? When he was a little baby, I carried him everywhere. Nobody thought that was the least bit strange. But now, he's over six feet tall and weighs a bit more than what he did when he was just six months old. If I walked around trying to carry Craig everywhere I went now, people would look at both of us and say, "There go a couple of nuts for you."

Yet, we have some Christians who are chronologically twenty or thirty years old in the Lord, and they expect to be carried by the pastor or the prayer group leader or someone else. It's time we grew up. If we want to be strong, mature Christians, we have to add power, or virtue, to our lives.

I sometimes wonder what some people would do if they were marooned on an island in the middle of the ocean somewhere — with no phones, no mail service, or anything. They couldn't call their pastor or the prayer group or the radio preacher. They couldn't write to anyone to help them out of their situation. They are going to have to learn how to talk to God for themselves and get their own answers. I wonder what would happen to those poor people.

Tapping Into God's Power

Thank goodness, God has given us a plan where we

can grow up — where we can mature spiritually. Where we, ourselves, can tap into the power of God. We do it by adding to our faith — virtue. In the days ahead, we are going to have to know how to use our own Christian energy to receive from God.

That's why Jesus told His disciples, ". . . *tarry ye in the city of Jerusalem, until ye be endued with power from on high*" (Luke 24:49). It is ridiculous to think that anybody is going to be a full-grown, spiritually-mature Christian without power. Without power, without virtue, you cannot stand against the tests and trials of the enemy.

Motivating Yourself With the Word

How do we add Christian energy, power, or virtue to our lives? By motivating ourselves with the Word of God. This is what fortifies our inner man. You see, energy is what motivates something to move. For example, let's say the enemy comes whispering in your ear, "You're a failure. You're never going to amount to anything. Who do you think you are anyway?"

What do we do with those lies? Unless we have added Christian energy to our faith and motivate ourselves with the Word of God, the devil will "whip us up one side and down the other," as we say down in Texas, where I come from.

What we need to do is begin speaking out God's Word, "*No, No, No!* Devil, you're a liar. I'm not listening

to you because greater is He who is in me than he who
is in the world. No weapon formed against me will pros-
per. I can do all things through Christ Jesus, who
strengthens me."

That's what I mean by motivating yourself with the
Word. You don't have to say too many of those verses
before you'll start feeling real good on the inside. Your
spirit man will rise up and begin to move.

You see, most people never get beyond the shouting
stage. But watch people who live on this emotional,
shouting plane stage. They never live the victorious life
that they're meant to live. They walk around like their
favorite dog just died or something. Ask them, "What's
wrong, brother?" and they'll give you a whole list of
their problems. "The devil's on my back! I don't know
what to do. I'm so discouraged." My answer to that is,
"Why don't you get the devil off your back then?" Use a
little virtue and energy that's on the inside of you and
get rid of him.

The Bible says, "*. . . Resist the devil, and he will flee
from you*" (James 4:7). Most Christians don't like to
resist. They don't want to expend any energy resisting.
And it does take energy. But, as I said earlier, most
Christians are basically lazy and want somebody else to
do it for them. We need to grow up and do it for ourselves.

Calling the Devil's Bluff

I remember when I was in the sixth grade, there was

this one guy who had been kept back a couple of years. He should have been in eighth grade but he was still back with all of us smaller guys. He towered over all of us — he was just a big, bad dude. If he caught you at your locker with your head in it, he'd slam that locker on your head as hard as he could. You'd pull your head out and wouldn't know where you were! Or you'd be walking down the aisle in some class and he'd stick his big foot out and trip you. You'd fall flat on your nose, and everybody would laugh at you.

This guy was just plain mean. Nobody liked him; we were all afraid of him. We'd all get together and talk about him, "I wish somebody would just get him." One day, I said to one of my friends, "Why don't you try it?" He said, "Oh, no, not me, how about you?" I said, "No way am I going to jump on him." We all talked like that and that was the problem — we were all talk and no action.

In our class there was this real quiet guy. He didn't say a whole lot, but when he did, you listened. If he'd had enough of something, you knew to listen to what he had to say, because he wouldn't say it twice.

I never will forget it. One day as we all headed out the door to recess, this big old boy knocked our quiet little friend down the steps. He sprawled flat out there in the dirt. Finally, he got up and turned around. Now, this guy who was so much bigger than us was standing towering above our friend. He was a couple of steps higher up and looked like a giant in comparison.

But our friend looked up at him and very calmly

said, "Don't you ever do that again." Well, this big guy just shoved him back down the steps and walked right over him. When he did that, our friend dove and hit the big guy. In one motion, he grabbed him by the legs and threw him on the ground and started hitting him with everything he was worth.

Left, right, left, right! Our friend just plowed into him. The rest of us all went wild, cheering him on. We caused such a commotion, some of the teachers came running over to break up the fight. The next thing we knew, the school principal came running up. We figured we were all in serious trouble.

As soon as the principal saw what was going on, he started to yell at everyone, "If any one of you doesn't like what's going on here, get back in the building now. I've been looking for someone to put this guy in his place for a long time. Now I've found him, and I'm not about to call him off." Well, that just egged all the rest of us on. That big bully got it but good. And we all had a ball cheering the fight on.

I learned something valuable that day, and I've never forgotten it. All that rough stuff that big bully was doing was a big bluff. We all thought he was so tough and mean. All it took was one person expending a little bit of energy, and that guy never pulled his bluff on anybody ever again! He'd walk down the hall and if it looked like he was even thinking of doing something mean, we'd all laugh at him, and say, "Remember what happened to you when our friend beat up on you? We'll do the same thing he did, so bug off." He never bothered any of us ever again!

We called his bluff. We learned he wasn't so big and mean after all. The devil's the same way; his main tactic is fear, trying to make us think he's a whole lot stronger than he actually is. He's already been defeated by Jesus. Jesus has already triumphed over him. But he's still running around trying to trip us up and bully us around.

If we'd just use a little bit of energy and tell him, "Listen, devil, my Elder Brother, Jesus, already beat you up and won, and I can too." Begin to quote the Word to him just like Jesus did when He was tempted.

MATTHEW 4:1-11
1   Then was Jesus led up of the spirit into the wilderness to be tempted of the devil.
2   And when he had fasted forty days and forty nights, he was afterward an hungred.
3   And when the tempter came to him, he said, If thou be the Son of God, command that these stones be made bread.
4   But he answered and said, "IT IS WRITTEN, Man shall not live by bread alone, but by every word that proceedeth out of the mouth of God.
5   Then the devil taketh him up into the holy city, and setteth him on a pinnacle of the temple,
6   And saith unto him, If thou be the Son of God, cast thyself down: for it is written, He shall give his angels charge concerning thee: and in their hands they shall bear thee up, lest at any time thou dash thy foot against a stone.
7   Jesus said unto him, IT IS WRITTEN again, Thou shalt not tempt the Lord thy God.
8   Again, the devil taketh him up into an exceeding high mountain, and sheweth him all the king-

doms of the world, and the glory of them;
9   And saith unto him, All these things will I give
thee, if thou wilt fall down and worship me.
10 Then saith Jesus unto him, Get thee hence,
Satan: for IT IS WRITTEN, Thou shalt worship the
Lord thy God, and him only shalt thou serve.
11 Then the devil leaveth him. . . .

Notice what Jesus did — He resisted the devil with
the Word of God. He called the devil's bluff. And what
happened? The devil left him. The devil knows he has
to back off. Call his bluff and he has to flee.

Our energy, our power, comes from the Word of God.
We need to use the tools that have been given to us to
maintain our maturity. The devil is beating up on people all the time because they don't want to get involved;
they don't want to expend a little energy resisting him
and speaking the Word of God. The devil loves lazy people because it just makes his job that much easier.

What would have happened if when Jesus was
tempted by the enemy, He had said, "Oh, this is too
hard! I can't resist the devil. I'm done for!" Fortunately
for all of us, that was not what Jesus did. Instead, He
rose up with the power within Him, spoke the Word of
God, resisted the enemy and called his bluff! Jesus
proved to us that Christian energy — virtue — is
unbeatable. It wins every time.

Virtue Equals Excellence

There is another meaning of virtue that we also need
to understand. *The Amplified Bible* calls virtue, *excel-*

lence — meaning excellence of character. If anybody needs to develop some excellence of character, it's Christians. Here you have someone who's supposed to be so big in faith, making all the right confessions, preaching faith, believing God for plush houses, big cars and fancy clothes, trying to look, "Oh, so spiritual." Then they go out and do something that is totally dishonest.

We need to develop moral integrity and excellence in every area of our lives. We need to develop excellence with one another. We had a RHEMA graduate who started a church in a certain town. The church was going along pretty well. Then another RHEMA graduate moved in and started another church just two blocks down the street. That's not Christian excellence. It's not ethically right; it's not the way of integrity.

Quality Pays

Excellence means something of valuable quality. That's the kind of people we should be.

Have you ever bought anything advertised as being "just like the original"? It's supposedly just like the original but a lot cheaper! So you go ahead and buy the cheaper brand instead of the name brand, thinking you're getting such a good deal! There's truth in that saying, "You get what you pay for."

It happens every year when you begin to have picnics and cookouts. You buy those flimsy paper plates because they're such a great deal. Then what happens?

You bring them home and start to put all the food on them — the potato salad, the macaroni salad, the beans, the coleslaw, and the fried chicken. The next thing you know the plate folds up on you, and you wind up with a lap full of food, and clothes covered with grease!

So you try to make the plates stronger by putting three or four of them together. You'd come out ahead to buy the more expensive quality plates to begin with. They may cost a little more initially, but they last longer so you save money in the long run. The sturdier, more expensive plates aren't inferior quality. Have you ever noticed that cheap merchandise doesn't hold up very long?

In a similar way, Christians should not be individuals of inferior quality. Jesus paid a great price for us. We're to be people of valuable quality — people of excellence. Add excellence to your faith. Add virtue to your faith, and your faith will be powerful. It will hold up when the going gets tough. With virtue in your life, no matter what circumstances or challenges come against you, you'll stand strong in faith — you'll hold up!

Firepower — Christian Energy Within

Before Peter says to add anything else to our faith, he first says to add virtue. Why is that so important? Because Peter knew that you would need power or Christian energy first. Why? To fight the battles of life. How are you going to fight the good fight of faith without any power or strength? Have you ever heard of an army going off to war without any firepower? Of course not. They wouldn't get very far without firepower.

That firepower or Christian energy is what will keep moving you forward when the going gets tough. The virtue or Christian energy that you develop is what will keep you going when the enemy comes in and tries to trip you up.

We are reaching a time on this earth when the devil is making his last all-out assault against the Church. Everything that can be shaken is going to be shaken. It will take those who know who they are in Christ and those who walk in *power — virtue — energy* — to stand against the wiles of the enemy, and keep on standing. You can live a victorious Christian life, but you can't do it without power — without adding virtue to your faith.

Chapter 3
Adding Knowledge:
Intelligent Spirituality

After adding virtue to our faith, Peter tells us to then add *knowledge*.

2 PETER 1:5
5 And beside this, giving all diligence, add to your faith virtue; and to virtue knowledge.

Knowledge can mean different things to different people. There's one word, however, that can be interchanged with knowledge; it's intelligence. *The Amplified Bible* actually uses the word "intelligence" for *knowledge* in this verse.

We need to add intelligence to our faith. I run into all kinds of people who are supposedly "in faith" yet are doing some of the dumbest things! If they'd just add a little bit of intelligence to their faith they'd be much better off than they are. You see, many people who say they are in faith are operating in foolishness or presumption. They may have a little bit of knowledge about faith, but they don't have any real intelligence concerning faith. Peter could have said, "What we need is some good ole intelligent spirituality."

I remember a young man who once worked for our ministry. He had some knowledge about cars, but no real intelligence concerning them. He could drive a car all right but that was all he knew about cars. One day his car blew up — it just totally blew up. He was driving along and the car started to smoke. The next thing he knew, it sounded like dynamite exploded underneath the hood, and the car just stopped dead in its tracks and blew up. He called a friend and said, "My car quit running and I don't know why. Can you come pick me up?"

Later, my Dad looked under the hood, and said, "Didn't you ever check the oil?" The car blew up because the guy never put any oil in it! The boy looked at Dad, and said, "I don't know anything about cars. Nobody told me to check the oil."

You see, he had some knowledge about the car. He did know how to drive it. He knew how to turn it on, put gas in it, how to turn the lights on, and how to stop it and turn it off. But that's about all he knew. He had no intelligence to combine with the knowledge he did have.

Intelligence is simply applying knowledge correctly. Anyone can amass all kinds of knowledge, but the real question is, "What are you doing with that knowledge?"

Use What You've Got

We need to quit chasing after more knowledge and use what we have. We need to know how to assimilate and use the knowledge we've already been given. A person who's really intelligent never quits acquiring knowledge until he breathes his last breath. He continues to go on learning more and more. But he does something with it.

People seem to always be searching for "deeper revelation." There isn't any deeper revelation than *"Use what you've got!"* People go around with what I call "itching ears." They just hear what they want to hear. A lot of people hear with the natural ear, but they never hear with the spiritual ear — the ear of the inner spirit man.

That's where problems arise. They go around saying, "I have the mind of Christ," and then go out and do things that give Christianity a bad reputation. They only listen to what they want to hear; they never really gain any intelligence. They never grow up.

As a parent, you set down certain rules for your children. When they're small, you'll tolerate some things that you won't allow when they get older. As they grow older you hold them accountable for more. God's the same way. He expects us to grow up and use some intelligence in our walk of faith.

Intelligence and God's Word

If you'll add intelligence to God's Word, you won't go around making foolish faith confessions that don't amount to anything. We need intelligence in exercising our faith. People who run around saying, "I confess this," "I claim that," and those things aren't even promised to them in the Bible, might as well be running around saying "Twinkle, twinkle little star," for all the good it's going to do them!

There is so much confusion about confessing God's Word where there shouldn't be. If people would just stick to God's Word, they wouldn't go wrong. The mistake a lot of people make is to "claim" other people's experiences rather than the promises in God's Word.

A brother in the Lord gave this testimony: "God told me to give my car away, so I did. Two weeks later, He gave me a brand-new car." Someone else heard that and decided he'd do the same thing. He gave his car away and began confessing, "God's going to give me a new car. God's going to give me a new car." He confessed that until he was blue in the face, but he ended up walking everywhere he went.

Was he confessing God's Word? *No.* He was confessing someone else's *experience.* The first guy heard from God; the second one did not. That's not using knowledge intelligently. He was not inspired by the Word of God. His confessions weren't based on the Word of God so they didn't work.

When their "faith" confessions don't work, many people go around whining and complaining, "This stuff doesn't work!" And they're absolutely right! It doesn't work unless you do it according to the Word of God — intelligently. It is not using intelligence to make faith confessions based on someone else's experiences or testimony. Experiences can get you in big trouble.

If something doesn't line up with the Word of God, be intelligent and throw it out. If we operate in intelligence, circumstances and experiences won't get the best of us. If you have a supernatural experience, judge it by God's Word. Then you won't get yourself into trouble.

The Bible says if we ask anything according to the will of God, He hears us and answers us (1 John 5:14,15). The key here is to ask according to His will. What is God's will? It is His Word. People go around making all kinds of so called "faith confessions" that have absolutely nothing to do with God's will or His Word. That's not intelligent.

We need intelligence when using our faith. I heard a story about someone who had been robbed a number of times. His house had been robbed; his car had been robbed; his office had been robbed. Every time the guy turned around, he was being robbed. All he said was, "I put the angels to work guarding my house and my car." Then he went off and left everything unlocked. That was not using intelligence.

Intelligence and Prosperity

Another area where we need more intelligence — where we need to add some knowledge to our faith — concerns prosperity. God does desire to bless His children. But if you're not tithing and giving, you can confess every prosperity scripture in the Bible until the Rapture and *it won't work for you*! You have to obey God's Word first before any confession will work.

If you're broke, that is a fact. To admit the fact that you are broke is not a bad confession. It's already a fact whether you ever put words to it or not. It won't do any good to go around saying, "I'm not broke! I'm not broke!" The fact is, you are. To say you aren't is really a lie.

What you should do is to start confessing God's Word, "I believe my God meets all my needs according to His riches in glory. My God delights in my prosperity. I'm seeking Him first so He shall add all things unto me." And then be intelligent and tithe and give!

You meet people who are obviously hurting about something, and you ask them how they are. Real quickly they'll reply, "Oh, great! I'm blessed. Everything's just wonderful!" They lied! If you are sick and hurting, it's a fact.

You're not out of faith by admitting the facts of something. You are *in faith* by applying the Word of God to it. This is what Abraham did. We could learn some things from his example. God had promised Abraham many descendents. In the natural, it looked impossible because both Abraham and his wife Sarah were beyond the age of childbearing. But Abraham was a man of faith.

ROMANS 4:19-21
19 And being not weak in faith, he considered not his own body now dead, when he was about an hundred years old, neither yet the deadness of Sarah's womb:
20 He staggered not at the promise of God through unbelief; but was strong in faith, giving glory to God;
21 And being fully persuaded that, what he had promised, he was able also to perform.

Without weakening in faith, Abraham faced the fact that his body was as good as dead, yet he did not waver through unbelief regarding the promise of God. But he was strengthened in his faith and gave glory to God.

Here's the key. Abraham was fully persuaded that God had power to do what He had promised. So the fact may be that you are sick, but there is a greater power than that fact — it's God's Word. Confess God's Word, not just some words of your own.

One man told me, "I'll never confess divorce in my family. It'll never happen." I said to him, "Sir, your wife has already been down to the courthouse; she's already filed for divorce. It's a fact, and all your confessing otherwise can't change that fact. You are divorced and that's that. Now begin to confess God's Word for a miracle."

Most people are running around confessing what they want and it doesn't have a thing to do with the Word of God. The Word of God is a gold mine. As you begin to dig in it, you find more and more treasures, and more and more promises. It's when you begin to dig on your own and study on your own, that the Word of God begins to be transferred from your head to your heart. Faith doesn't work in the head, it works in the heart.

But people are lazy. They just want to sit and listen to this preacher and that preacher. People run all over the country going from one seminar to the next, hoping for some new truth to be revealed. They never dig into the Word of God for themselves.

The Bible says to study to show yourself approved (2 Tim. 2:15)! We need to study; we need to acquire more knowledge. But then we need to apply that knowledge intelligently. We can have an educated head *and* an educated heart. When you put the two together, you become an explosive force for God.

Intelligence and Healing

Another area where we need to apply some intelligence concerns healing. A few years ago at Campmeeting, an individual was wheeled in all hooked up to various machines. Those machines were keeping this person alive until he could sit under the Word of God and believe God for his healing.

As soon as they wheeled him in, some "faith nut" ran over and began yanking all the wires and everything off of him, saying, "The power of God is in this place." The person in the wheelchair almost died because of one person's stupidity. That was not using faith intelligently. That person may have meant well, but they were going about it all wrong.

When it comes to healing, people have all kinds of crazy ideas. They don't use their faith intelligently. Some people think if you throw your medicine away, that's what will heal you. No, it's God's Word and power that will heal you. Throwing away your medicine is not what's going to heal you. Do you have faith in God's Word, or is your faith in throwing away the medicine? Some people seem to have more faith in throwing their medicine away; they think that's what's going to heal them rather than God's Word. Then they get in big trouble.

I know a preacher who was a diabetic. He'd been a diabetic for thirty-two years. Every morning, he checked his insulin level and gave himself an injection. The doctors had told him that he'd have to do that for his entire life. But then he began to hear about God's healing power. Then every morning when he gave himself that shot, he started confessing, "I thank my God for His healing in my body. By His stripes I have been healed. The power of God is working in my body to effect a healing and a cure. He sent His Word and healed me." He'd continue to confess different healing scriptures over himself every day.

Notice, he didn't quit taking his medicine and run around confessing, "I don't have diabetes anymore. I don't have diabetes." No, he confessed God's Word over the situation. Guess what happened? He went in for a checkup and his doctor told him, "You don't need insulin anymore. You're healed."

This preacher used his faith intelligently. We need to realize that medical science is available to help us, not hurt us.

Sometime ago, there was a story in the newspaper about a young boy, only nine years old, who died from a ruptured appendix. That is a horrible way to die. The parents said, "Our church is against doctors and against medicine." So they let their little boy die. That boy's death was totally unnecessary. Now there's a law in some states that parents have to seek medical care for their children or they can be tried for manslaughter.

There's nothing wrong with going to a doctor. They're fighting the same fight we're fighting — we're just doing it through divine means, and they're going about it through natural means. If someone's sick, it doesn't really matter how they get well just so long as they get well. I say, let's use everything at our disposal.

Working With the Doctors

We went through a very critical illness several years ago with my son, Craig. He had a problem that needed immediate medical attention. There was a tumor on his brain! The doctors told us we couldn't wait; he needed surgery immediately. We were all praying about what to do, and my Dad told me, "No army ever went out to fight without a second line of defense. If their first plan doesn't work, they always have a second line of defense to fall back on."

He said, "A lot of times people get whipped in the first round of a fight, but they don't quit. They come back and win. Just because you don't make the connection in the first round, don't quit. Fall back, regroup, and then come out fighting again."

That's exactly what we did. We prayed and took Craig in for the surgery, believing God for a totally successful surgery and a complete and quick recovery. We prayed for the doctors. Everything we did, we did in faith. That medical help saved my boy's life while we stood in faith. We didn't let down in our faith. We just sought a little additional help from the doctors, and there's nothing wrong with that. It is not a sign of how spiritual you are by whether or not you go to a doctor.

Craig was in surgery for 12 hours. One of the nurses told us later, "The power of God was in that operating room. I've been believing God for healing in my back, and my healing was totally manifested during that operation."

We prayed and believed God for a perfect operation with no complications. And that's what we got. After the surgery, the doctor told us everything went perfectly, but that the bone in Craig's skull would never grow back completely. We all prayed and believed God that it would grow back and be just as it was before.

When Craig went out for freshman football, they wouldn't allow him to play until he had a CAT scan of his brain to make sure everything was all right. He went through a whole series of tests and they came back *perfect*. Even the bone had grown back perfectly!

You see, we did our part, and the doctors did theirs. We were all working toward the same goal — Craig's total recovery. We don't have to work against doctors. Let them do their jobs. Our job is to stand in faith — intelligently.

I've seen people come for prayer in healing lines. They ask for prayer for their eyes and then immediately turn around and go stomp on their glasses. Then they go outside and try to drive and cause an accident because they haven't received the full manifestation of healing in their eyes yet. That's not using faith very intelligently.

The intelligent thing to do would be to continue to confess your healing every time you put those glasses on. When it comes, you'll know it. You won't be able to see out of those glasses anymore. Then go stomp on them if that's what makes you happy.

I know a lady in California who did this. Every time she put her glasses on she'd say, "Thank You, God, for Your healing power that's working in my eyes. Thank You, God, for 20-20 eyesight, for You restore my youth like the eagle's." After about six months, she couldn't see when she put her glasses on anymore. When she went in for an eye test, the doctor told her, "You don't need these glasses anymore. Take them off. Your eyes are perfect."

All good things come from God whether it is through divine or natural means (James 1:17). Just continue to stand in faith until the healing comes. Medicine and faith can work in harmony with each other for a complete cure if we'll just be intelligent about it.

Intelligence and the Holy Spirit

Another area where we need intelligence is in the operation of the gifts of the Spirit — particularly where it concerns the vocal gifts of the Spirit. The vocal gifts include tongues, interpretation of tongues, and prophecy.

Tongues, the interpretation of tongues, and the simple

gift of prophecy all do the same thing. They exhort, comfort and edify. That's their purpose. If a word comes forth that doesn't do one of these three things, then it's not the Spirit of God.

Lots of times, people's flesh and emotions get involved. Even though they say, "Thus saith the Lord," it's not a true "Thus saith the Lord." It's just their own flesh or emotions. We need to be sensitive to the Spirit and be intelligent about His gifts.

I heard a story about a lady who jumped up and supposedly began to prophesy at a prayer meeting. She said, "Thus saith the Lord, 'Don't be afeard little children. But if you do get afeard, don't worry, because sometimes I get afeard, too!'"

That was no more the Lord than the man in the moon! How do you know it was wrong? It doesn't line up with the Word of God. Where in the Word of God does it ever say that God is afraid? Any interpretation or prophecy that doesn't line up with the Word of God is wrong! That's all there is to it.

When a preacher is in the pulpit preaching, and the anointing is on him as the leader of the meeting, it is wrong for someone to jump up in the middle of his preaching and interrupt him with a tongue or prophecy. That person in the pulpit is anointed by the Holy Spirit. And the Holy Spirit wouldn't interrupt Himself to speak. He is a Gentleman — not the author of confusion! The Holy Spirit never interrupts Himself.

Everything is to be done decently and in order, Paul told us (1 Cor. 14:40). We need to use some intelligence with these vocal gifts of the Spirit.

I remember a crusade meeting we held in Detroit several years ago. It was outside in a big tent and there were about 3,500 people there inside the tent, plus a lot of people standing outside. It was a powerful meeting. The anointing was really strong and my Dad was right in the middle of an altar call. The Spirit was really moving in that place, convicting people of sin. About 800 or 900 people came forward to be saved.

My Dad was exhorting the people at the altar, and all of a sudden a woman jumped up in the congregation and began to shout. Some of our ushers went over to her immediately, and said, "Sister! Sister! Calm down. Be quiet now. Just hold that." She just looked at them and said, "I can't hold it. When the Spirit moves, I can't stop it." And she began to shout louder. So our ushers took her by the arms and escorted her out of the tent.

Someone rebuked them, saying, "Hey, you quenched the Spirit!" That's right, they did — the wrong spirit!

There has been such misuse and abuse of the vocal gifts of the Spirit; many people have totally quenched any move of the Spirit for fear that things would get out of control. Now that's what grieves the Spirit of God. We just need to use intelligence in these things. Don't just shut it all down because a few people make mistakes. Most people mean well, but they're just not experienced yet. Teach them, and show them the right way to do things.

I remember sitting in a congregation one time listening to another minister preach. The Spirit began to move on me in a strong way. It was so powerful in me, I could barely contain it. It got to where I thought I would explode with this prophecy inside me. I just kept waiting for the minister in charge to give an opportunity for the Spirit to move.

When I realized he wasn't going to, I sat there and prayed. Now I didn't pray out loud. I sat there with my eyes wide open watching him, and I prayed silently, "Lord, I'm not going to interrupt this man. I know that's wrong and not in order. But I believe this is from You, so do something to give this word an opportunity to come forth. Either get him to stop so I can give it, or give it to him to deliver."

I no sooner got those thoughts out than the man in the pulpit began to speak the same word that was inside me. He began speaking it out in his preaching. The minute he did, it lifted from me. You see, he was sensitive to the Spirit of God, too. We need to use some intelligence when it comes to the operation of the vocal gifts.

Sometimes you'll be preaching, and the simple gift of prophecy will begin to operate right in the middle of your preaching. It will come forth under a strong anointing to exhort, edify, and comfort people. I have had this happen several times while preaching.

One thing we need to learn is that God is not going to do things the same way every time. He doesn't have to climb into our boxes or jump through our hoops. God is not going to move the same way every time we step inside the church. He's God. He can do whatever He wants, when He wants. But He will do it in line with His Word.

If you receive a prophecy or a tongue in a service, hold it until the leader of that service gives you the opportunity to give it forth. If that opportunity never comes, and it really was the Spirit of God, you won't be held accountable for it; that leader will. The person in charge of that meeting will be held accountable because he should be sensitive to the Spirit. But don't interrupt a meeting just so you can speak. If it's a true, "Thus saith the Lord," a time will come to give it.

Tongues and Interpretation

If you have a tongue to give, also pray for the interpretation of that tongue (1 Cor. 14:13). The Bible very clearly states that no tongue should be given without an interpretation (1 Cor. 14:26-28). That just causes confusion.

Years ago, I traveled as crusade director for my Dad. I'd feel the Spirit moving on me, so I'd step forward and give a message in tongues, and then step back and wait for him to interpret it.

One night after a service, he said to me, "Don't ever give a message in tongues again unless you intend to interpret it, because I'm not going to bail you out anymore." And he didn't either!

I learned quickly to make sure it was definitely a true message in tongues from the Holy Spirit, and not just me. I also made sure that I had the interpretation for it. If people would be held accountable to give the interpretation for every message in tongues they give, there'd be a lot less confusion. It would also cut out a lot of so-called tongues that aren't inspired by the Spirit at all!

Sometimes people give out a message in tongues when they should keep quiet and simply pray to themselves in tongues. There's a big difference between tongues for personal prayer and tongues as a gift of the Spirit to be given forth in a congregation.

One last thing concerning these vocal gifts. If a prophecy comes forth that doesn't bear witness with your spirit and doesn't confirm something you already know — don't accept it. I've known of people who came to RHEMA based on a prophecy they got from someone, telling them they were called into ministry. Then they failed in the ministry and wondered why. They were never called into the ministry in the first place. *God* calls a person into ministry on a personal basis, not through some prophecy. All prophecy does is confirm what a person already knows in his spirit.

Helping People

The Bible says God's people perish for lack of knowledge (Hosea 4:6). We have lacked knowledge in the moving of the vocal gifts of the Spirit. We need to add intelligence to their operating in our midst. If we will allow the gifts to operate intelligently, people will genuinely be helped. That's the bottom line — helping people. The gifts aren't given to make someone look spiritual; they're given to help people.

There's a story about a prayer meeting where a woman jumped up and prophesied, "So-and-so, won't be here tonight." This woman knew that because she'd just spoken with that person on the phone before coming to the meeting. Then a couple of minutes later this same woman happened to glance out the window and saw a certain car driving up, so she jumped up again and prophesied, "So-and-so changed his mind. Pretty soon he'll be knocking at the door, 'Thus saith the Lord!'"

What was she doing? She was attempting to use the gifts of the Spirit to look spiritual. That's an abuse and misuse of the gifts of the Spirit. We need to grow up and use intelligence or knowledge in every area of our lives — in faith, confession, healing, prosperity and the gifts of the Spirit.

Add intelligence — add knowledge to our faith. That's what Peter said to do. We need to quit chasing after new revelation and intelligently use the revelations we already have been given.

Possessing knowledge is more than knowing information and facts; it requires an understanding of the information and the ability to apply that information. Peter said, "If these things be in you and abound, you shall not be unfruitful in the knowledge of our Lord Jesus Christ" (2 Peter 1:8).

Nobody in their right mind wants to be unfruitful in their knowledge of God. Every Christian would be quick to say that they want to know more of Jesus. But knowing more about Jesus comes from doing some things with our faith. Doing what things? Adding virtue first and then adding knowledge. Knowledge of God will increase as it is acted upon.

Chapter 4
Adding Temperance: Controlling Self

Let's review our original text for a moment.

2 PETER 1:3-6
3 According as his divine power hath given unto us all things that pertain unto life and godliness, through the knowledge of him that hath called us to glory and virtue:
4 Whereby are given unto us exceeding great and precious promises: that by these ye might be partakers of the divine nature, having escaped the corruption that is in the world through lust.
5 AND BESIDE THIS, GIVING ALL DILIGENCE, ADD TO YOUR FAITH virtue; and to virtue knowledge;
6 And to knowledge temperance. . . .

After adding virtue and knowledge to our faith, the next character quality we need is temperance. Temperance simply means self-control. Someone possessing temperance in his life is marked by moderation in actions, thoughts, and feelings. Someone with temperance knows how to restrain his body and soul (his mind, will, and emotions), and keep them in subjection to his spirit.

It's not an easy thing to always be self-controlled. Self is always wanting to rise up, isn't it? In this day and age in which we live, people generally don't know how to exercise self-control. It's not something that is being taught to a great extent. Temperance is not a well-liked word in our world today.

For a long time, we lived through what we called the "me" generation. The prevailing attitude was: "What's in it for me?" That's a very selfish attitude, but it's very easy to be selfish. It's a lot harder to be self-controlled, because it means being self-less. Less of self is hard to attain.

Many people have never learned self-control in the natural, and as a result, it's very difficult for them to have any self-control in the spiritual areas of life.

I've met some young men who refuse to date because they say they can't control themselves. They've said to me, "I'm afraid I'll go too far with a girl." I realize this is a touchy subject, but these things are going on in the Church, and it's about time we dealt with them honestly. Otherwise we'll never help these young men.

I've actually had some of them ask me, "Please pray that God will take these desires away from me." I tell them, "I can't do that." It's a foolish request, because God made men with a desire for women and He made women, with a desire for men. God's Word says that it is not good for man to be alone. That's why we have those desires. It's God's design. If I pray that God takes away those desires, then the devil could come in and give them unnatural desires that would be much worse!

What I tell them is this, "You need to learn some self-discipline — some self-control. Develop temperance in your life, Brother." If the young men who come to me with these problems would just develop temperance, they could date with no problem. I've had some say, "I just don't have self-control."

That's a lie. If you are a born-again Christian, you have temperance in your life because it's a fruit of the spirit. And every believer has all nine fruits of the spirit in them (Gal. 5:22,23). It's just that some people walk through life with those fruits operating in and through them more than others do.

Some of us have more victory in certain areas of our lives than in other areas. We all have areas that need improvement. For example, I happen to come from a line of people by the name of "Hagin." Every one that I know who has that name is high-strung. They all have a high-powered, "go-get-'em" type attitude. They also have a fuse that's very short. In other words, they have a temper.

It's easy for me to say, "Well, that's just the way I am because I'm a Hagin, and we're all short-tempered," as an excuse for behavior that's not right.

I remember a few years back when I went out to play golf after not playing in a long time. It was evident that I hadn't been playing regularly. I hit the ball with a nine iron club and the ball went in every direction except the one I wanted it to go. I grabbed that nine iron, went over to the nearest tree, and pounded that poor tree with my nine iron. I bent the nine iron all to pieces.

Then I realized that little eyes next to me were watching every move I made. I turned to my son who was about four years old then, and said, "Don't tell

Momma." What happened? The first thing he did when he walked through the door was to run up to his mother and exclaim, "Guess what I saw Daddy do today, Momma!"

Children will teach you how to be self-controlled real fast! I realized I had to get a grip on self-control in my life. It's not something you get control of once, either. It's something you've got to work at continually, every day.

Self-control means discipline. If you don't discipline yourself daily in prayer, in reading God's Word, in going to church, in your finances, on your job, in your family, and so on, the pressures will get to you. Without discipline, as those pressures pile up, you'll walk around ready to explode.

Almost every time I used to go out on the golf course, I'd explode, damage some poor tree, and destroy my clubs. Everybody used to laugh at me. It got to be a joke to see how long I could go without exploding. That's sad. But I finally reached the point where I didn't explode anymore, and I could enjoy my game even if it wasn't so great.

It wasn't easy at first. I'd hit a ball and it would go the wrong way, and I'd grit my teeth singing something like, "What a friend we have in Jesus." But it got easier and easier. If I started to feel anger rising in me, I started to quote Scripture. I took that anger and by applying the Word to gain self-control in my game, it made me a better player.

Controlling Anger

If you have a short temper, don't condemn yourself for it. Just get it under control. Somehow preachers have given the impression that anger is wrong. So no one expresses it; they just keep it all pent up inside. They just hold it in and then one day, it explodes.

It's interesting to see just how much the Bible says about anger. God got angry in plenty of places. Anger takes up three whole pages in the *Strong's Exhaustive Concordance of the Bible*!

Jesus got angry too. He didn't just tiptoe into the temple and ask the buyers and sellers there to leave whenever it was convenient for them. The Bible tells us that he went in there and threw them out along with their money tables (Mark 11:15,16).

We need to learn how to have self-control in line with God's Word. When He saw the house of the Lord being defiled, Jesus got mad. So mad in fact, that He drove those people out. Was Jesus happy and smiling while doing that? No, He was angry, very angry.

But Jesus controlled that anger and did something productive with it. A lot of people say it's wrong to ever get upset or angry. That's not true. God made us with emotions; they're not bad. He gave them to us for a purpose. We just need to learn how to control them and make them work for us. Then they will lead us to victory, not defeat.

If the Father and Jesus could get angry, it's obvious that anger isn't quite the horrible, dreaded sin we thought it was. Anger's not the real problem — it's what we do with it that causes the problem (Eph. 4:26,27). We need to learn to express our anger in positive ways. By that, I mean we must channel it properly.

Every now and then you read some horrible story in the newspaper about someone who goes out and kills several people. The murderer will plead insanity and say, "I couldn't help it. I just got mad and something got hold of me and made me do it." They have no self-control, so they pass the blame.

As a Christian, however, we do have self-control. It is in us. How much self-control we have is up to us.

I heard a story about someone who worked in a grocery store at the check-out counter. One day a customer came through his line, and the grocery clerk jumped across the counter and started trying to cast a devil out of the customer. Of course, he was immediately fired. When they asked him why he did it, he said, "Oh, God came on me, and I just couldn't help myself."

He blamed God for his own lack of self-control. That was the wrong time and place to go doing those kinds of things. God had nothing to do with it. You can control the Spirit of God on the inside of you. He won't make you do anything you don't want to do — especially anything that causes a spectacle and makes you and Him look foolish.

The reason we have so many problems in some of our churches today is that people are running around uncontrolled with no real discipline in their lives. You start talking about discipline and people say, "Oh, that's bondage." There's a big difference between bondage and self-control.

Paul said he kept his body under and brought it into subjection (1 Cor. 9:27). In other words, he kept himself in control. Let me say it again; God won't make you do anything *if you don't want to*. He prompts and He gently leads or urges you. He doesn't force you to do anything. You are the one in control. It is the enemy who pushes people to do things, not God.

Paul said, ". . . *the spirits of the prophets are subject to the prophets*" (1 Cor. 14:32). What does that mean? It means you are always in control. People who jump up all the time in the middle of a service to give tongues or prophecies, saying that they can't control it, are wrong. They can control it; they just don't want to. Or maybe they are just operating in ignorance. We need to have some self-control when it comes to the gifts of the Spirit.

Controlled by the Word

Temperance means self-control. It's showing restraint over your own impulses, actions, thoughts, words, and desires. You can control yourself. But you're not going to be able to control yourself without help. You do it through the Word of God. It's the Word of God that renews your mind and helps you to live a controlled life.

This is why it's so important to have a regular, daily Bible reading program. It will help you develop self-control. When something happens and you feel like you're about to explode, if the Word is in you, it will rise up and stop you. *"He that is slow to anger is better than the mighty; and he that ruleth his spirit than he that taketh a city"* (Prov. 16:32).

Let's say something happens and you're sorely tempted to lose your patience. The Word of God, if it's in you, will remind you, *". . . let patience have her perfect work . . ."* (James 1:4).

The key is to make sure that the Word of God is *in* you. Sometimes things are too easy for us today. We have books and tapes and seminars that often take the place of reading the Word of God for ourselves. We need to read and study the Word daily for ourselves in order to develop self-control. No one else can do it for us. And we can't blame anyone else if we don't have self-control.

Temperance With Other People

I've had to learn self-control in dealing with my staff. Oftentimes, I see things that get me irritated. I want things done a certain way and when they're not done the way I've asked, it bugs me. Over the years, I've learned a lot about how to deal with those irritations and frustrations. I don't chew people out like I used to.

You know what most of us do? When things don't go exactly the way we think they should, we want to grab people and jerk them up to our level. We want to force them to receive our level of faith. But if we have any self-control, we'll climb down the pinnacle we think we're on and find out where they are. We'll find out where we can agree with them and work with them on their level. Then we can gently work at bringing them up to our level.

It can be especially frustrating for pastors to see people who never seem to want to grow up. You want to grab them and make them grow up overnight, or else! More people are helped by being loved up to another level of spirituality than they are by being condemned and criticized in frustration and anger.

Godly Discipline With Love

My grandmother knew what it meant to use the strap of discipline. She stood five feet eleven inches tall and could pick more cotton than most men could.

When I stayed with her and did something wrong, sometimes she'd just correct me with love. Then there were other times when she'd walk out into the back-yard and make herself a "peach tree switch." She'd take a butcher knife and cut one of the limbs off the peach tree.

I don't think there's anything that hurts worse than one of those little old peach tree switches. If you've never had the privilege of being disciplined with one of them, then you've missed out. It stings and leaves welts on your legs.

My grandmother knew exactly how to discipline me to get results. It would be a good long time before I'd do something else that required another switching, believe me!

Was my grandmother being mean to me? No, she disciplined me because she loved me. God's the same way. If we don't discipline ourselves, He will.

God does discipline us. He chastens us because He loves us. *"For whom the Lord loveth he chasteneth . . ."* (Heb. 12:6). But God doesn't chasten us, or discipline us like some people think — by putting curses on us or making us sick to teach us something.

God disciplines and chastens us by His Word (2 Tim. 3:16,17). If we would discipline ourselves, and judge ourselves, God wouldn't have to. For example, God told Hezekiah to put his house in order. Hezekiah turned his face to the wall, repented, and cried out to God, "Lord, I'm sorry. Don't judge me. Forgive me and I'll change." The Lord said, "All right, I'm going to give you fifteen more years simply because you turned to Me" (2 Kings 20:1-6).

As a parent, haven't you ever meted out judgment to one of your children and then later changed it? Your child comes to you and says, "Dad, I'm sorry. I really should have known better than to do that, and I won't do it again, I promise. I know I deserve to be grounded [or whatever punishment you decide upon] but there are some special activities coming up the next few weeks at school, and I really need to be involved in them. I know you've given me justice, Dad, but I need some mercy."

Oftentimes when your children do that with the

right heart, you'll show them some mercy. You'll back off and be a little more lenient and you'll say, "Okay, let's work something else out as punishment then."

God's like that, too. He is a God of mercy *to those who will judge themselves*. But He's also a God of justice and discipline. You can't just go around doing whatever you want to do and not expect to reap some consequences. Discipline is not bondage. Our own lack of discipline and self-control is what leads us into bondage.

Disciplining the Body

Sometimes if we'd be more diligent in exercising self-control, we wouldn't have to come to God for healing so much. People come up in healing lines all the time for prayer for stomach disorders such as ulcers. They're not eating properly. They're pushing themselves beyond their limits, not getting enough sleep, not praying or reading the Word of God, and worrying all the time. No wonder they have ulcers. If they'd just exercise a little self-control, they wouldn't have those problems.

What about people who come up and say, "Pray for me that I'll lose weight. Cast the spirit of gluttony out of me." Then they leave the service where they were just prayed for and go eat huge quantities of food at the nearest restaurant they can find. They sit down and pray, "I cast all the calories out of this food." That is foolishness! They need to exercise self-control and do some "push aways" — "push aways" from the table!

Stay in the Boat

Teaching about self-control doesn't exactly cause people to dance and shout! But we need to share this truth with the people in our churches so they will grow. Another way I like to talk about self-control is to say, "Stay in the boat."

Have you ever been in a small boat when one person stood up? The boat begins to rock a little bit, but if everyone just stays calm and still, the boat will usually come back under control.

Sometimes what happens is that everyone gets excited when the boat starts to rock just a little bit. They're afraid the boat is going to turn over, so they get up and start moving around. Before you know it, the boat tips over and everyone in it falls out. If they'd just exercised a little self-control and rode the waves out, they'd have been fine.

I see the same thing happen in churches. A little ripple, a problem of some kind, comes up and the church starts to rock a little bit. Some people can't contain their excitement, and they jump ship. If they'd just stay steady and just exercise a little self-control, things would work out. People are quick to take sides when a problem arises.

Usually the truth isn't on either side completely; the full truth usually falls right in the middle somewhere. The best thing we can do in a circumstance like that is to keep our tongues quiet and pray for the situation.

Controlling the Tongue

The easy thing to do when everything's not going just perfect is to talk about it to anyone who will listen. It often seems that Christians have more problems with gossip than just about anything else. We may not be guilty of the big sins like murder, adultery, drunkenness and so on, but when it comes to gossiping, we're in a lot of trouble. Did you know that God hates gossip because it sows discord (Prov. 6:16-19)?

The Bible has much to say about controlling our tongues:

PROVERBS 10:19
19 In the multitude of words there wanteth not sin: but he that refraineth his lips is wise.

PROVERBS 11:9
9   An hypocrite with his mouth destroyeth his neighbor: but through knowledge shall the just be delivered.

PROVERBS 18:6-8
6   A fool's lips enter into contention, and his mouth calleth for strokes.
7   A fool's mouth is his destruction, and his lips are the snare of his soul.
8   The words of a talebearer are as wounds, and they go down into the innermost parts of the belly.

PROVERBS 21:23
23 Whoso keepeth his mouth and his tongue keepeth his soul from troubles.

James tells us that if we can control our tongue, we can control our whole body (James 3:2). What a promise! The best way we can control ourselves is to control our tongue. The only way to do that effectively is to control it with the Word of God. Speak forth the Word instead of what just pops into your thinking. It will help you to live a self-controlled — a temperate life. If we add temperance to our faith, our faith will be a lot more effective.

Chapter 5

Adding Patience: Endurance That Refuses To Quit

Peter told us to add temperance to our lives before he said anything about patience. Actually, the two go hand in hand; you can't really have one without the other. Temperance or self-control, however, has to come first because without self-control, you'll never be able to develop patience. It takes self-control to be patient.

Patience means steadfastness. Someone who is patient knows how to endure. They're stable no matter what happens. The reason some people never receive anything from God is that they are not patient. They can't endure anything, and they give up too easily.

James says, ". . . *that the trying of your faith worketh patience*" (James 1:3). The trying of your faith implies there will be some things to endure. Read about Paul's, Peter's, or James' life. Those men knew what it meant to endure. They faced stonings, beatings, and all kinds of persecutions and opposition. But they knew how to believe God. They kept their faith in God. And the power and grace of God was sufficient to see them through every difficulty victoriously. They came out conquerors.

Timothy said, ". . . *what persecutions I endured: but out of them all the Lord delivered me*" (2 Tim. 3:11). Some people seem to think if they'll just walk by faith, they'll never have another problem, trial, trouble, or tribulation as long as they live. Are they ever in for a surprise! I don't know what kind of faith they have, but it's not the Bible kind of faith. It's not the faith we find in God's Word.

The minute you start to walk by faith and believe God's Word, the devil's going to come to find out if you really believe what you say, or if you're just all talk.

There are a lot of people who are all talk. They can *talk* a pretty good fight, but they can't really *fight* the good fight of faith. They quit as soon as things get the least bit tough. Their faith is weak. When it comes right down to it, they have no endurance — no patience to endure the hard times. But patience and endurance in the hard times is what develops true, strong faith.

That's why James said to "*. . . count it all joy when ye fall into divers temptations; Knowing this, that the trying of your faith worketh patience. But let patience have her perfect work, that ye may be perfect and entire, wanting nothing*" (James 1:2-4).

You see, you can count it joy because you know that as you endure and stand firm in faith, your faith is going to become stronger. You are not rejoicing over the problem or thanking God for the trial. You are thanking Him and rejoicing in the fact that He is going to deliver you out of it. And you will come through it stronger.

No one has ever received anything from God in the natural or in the spiritual realm without showing some endurance. You can't succeed at anything without endurance — without patience. Some people seem to think that faith is a get-rich-quick scheme. It's not. Real faith knows what it means to be patient and endure until the answer comes.

The reason some people never receive answers from God is that they quit too soon. About the time the answer is ready to reach them, they lose patience and quit trusting God. Their faith runs out.

The Bible says that it is through faith *and patience* that we inherit the promises (Heb. 6:12). Everyone likes the faith part, but they want to throw out the patience part. They just want to cut that little word "patience" right out of their Bibles!

Success in prayer only comes through patience. Daniel learned this, and we can learn from his experience. Remember the time when Daniel prayed and then waited, . . . and waited, . . . and waited. He waited twenty-one days before ever receiving an answer. If Daniel was like the rest of us, I'm sure he was wondering what was taking so long! Then an angel came, and it's interesting to note what that angel said.

> **DANIEL 10:12**
> **12 Then said he unto me, Fear not, Daniel: FOR FROM THE FIRST DAY that thou didst set thine heart to understand, and to chasten thyself before thy God, thy words were heard, and I am come for thy words.**

From *the very first day*, Daniel's prayer was heard. When the angel finally arrived, Daniel probably wanted to say, "Where in the world have you been? Don't you know I've been here waiting?" The angel told him that it was the prince of Persia (a demonic ruler in the heavenlies) that had held him up. The angel had to wrestle to get through to Daniel with the answer to his prayer (Dan. 10:12,13).

For twenty-one days, Daniel waited. It was Daniel's steadfastness — his patience that ensured the answer. Many times we rob ourselves of the answer because we throw in the towel right before our answer comes. We lose all the ground we ever gained by quitting too soon. Stay patient. Stay steadfast. Endure until the answer comes.

The problem is that we want everything handed to us on a silver platter. We always want the easy way out. Stay in there when the going gets rough. Don't quit. You'll find out what kind of character you have when life calls for patience and endurance.

Harry Truman once said, "The way you endure that which you must endure is more important than the crisis itself."

Commitment Takes Patience

Many can talk a good talk. But when the chips are down, you find out whether you have the real commitment needed to stand in there and fight to the finish. When the going gets rough, those who are just mouthing things won't last. Those kind of people are gone when things begin to heat up. Those with commitment will stick. Stick-to-it-tive-ness is another good word for patience or endurance.

In this day and age, it's easy to not be committed to anything. People go here and there just looking for a good time. They like to shout and get excited about faith, healing, prosperity, and all the blessings of God. But they don't want to stick around to hear anything serious like commitment, sin, tithing, or developing character. Those people are the first to declare that discipline is bondage! That is not true, but I'll tell you what *will* produce bondage. If you don't know the full counsel of God, you will definitely wind up in bondage!

People run around saying, "Give me more! Give me more! Give me more! I want more revelation." They don't care if it's truth or not. They're not even disciplined in what they listen to or under what teaching they sit. If a "revelation" doesn't line up with God's Word, we have no business having anything to do with it. But some people aren't even self-controlled enough to know the difference. They haven't disciplined their spirit man to be sensitive to truth or to error, so they'll just swallow anything.

People like that remind me of little birds with their beaks wide open, just waiting for the momma bird to fly up and drop something in. It doesn't matter what she gives them; they'll take anything. An attitude like that will cause people to be out of balance.

I'll tell you how to determine who the really committed people are in your church. Start a building program! As soon as you mention a building program, you see immediately who the truly committed ones are. Most people leave quickly and you never see them

again until the building's all finished. Then they myste-
riously pop back up again, and say, "Oh, what a great
building we have built!" You want to shake them, and
say, "That *who* built? Just exactly where were you when
we were working on this building?"

They don't want to be there when it calls for commitment, patience, endurance, or steadfastness. They just
want to be there for the exciting times — the goose-
bumps. They don't stick around when the going gets a
little tough. They have no commitment.

If you want to be a success at anything, you have to
make a commitment to the things of God. Pastors, it
doesn't matter whether there are three people out in
your congregation or 3,000. I learned a long time ago if
there are just three people out there, you preach like
there are 3,000 present.

You need to examine yourself, and ask, "Why am I
doing what I'm doing?" It all comes back to what God
told you to do. If God said do it, you do it, no matter
how many people are there. You brace yourself with a
backbone of steel, and you stand and deliver the Word
of God in the hard places. If you make a commitment to
go with God, you have to live up to that commitment.

People don't want to talk about commitment or
steadfastness. We live in the great microwave generation — fast food, fast banking, fast cars, fast sleeping,
fast working, fast everything. The truth is that we are
basically impatient in our everyday lives, and it carries
over into our spiritual lives.

If we have to stand in line at the grocery store for

more than three minutes we start getting impatient. We get over into the express lane where we're only supposed to have ten items. We look at the guy in front of us and start counting his items. If he's got more than ten items we start fuming and think, *Hey you! You're not supposed to be in this line. You're taking up my time, Buddy.*

How many of us have done that? Sometimes we even get upset with God. Why? Because we're impatient. It's something we need to change.

Measuring Your Patience

One of the main ways you can tell how spiritually mature you are is by measuring your level of patience. When someone is sick, you put a thermometer in his mouth to measure his temperature. Some of us need to measure our patience. Are we at the zero mark or have we progressed to a higher degree of patience?

One good way to measure our patience is by our reaction to unsaved loved ones. If they're not getting saved as quickly as we'd like, what do we usually do? We jump in and try to make it happen. Then we mess things up.

If we don't see something happening immediately, we start getting impatient. Then we begin speaking all kinds of doubt and unbelief. We nullify our prayers for them through impatience.

We tear down everything that's already been built up through our prayers by doubt, unbelief, and lack of patience.

Without great patience, there is no great faith. Without great faith, there are no great victories. You won't achieve any victory without a battle. That's why the Christian walk is called the fight of faith.

Nobody wins if they don't get in the fight. You can't win any fight by sitting down on the sidelines, saying, "Gee, I hope our team wins today. I'll just sit over here and watch." No, someone has to get in there and make a commitment to the team and get involved.

Have you ever watched a basketball or football game? Those coaches and managers have to learn to exercise a lot of patience. At times it looks like there's no way their team can win but the coach patiently sticks with his team. He doesn't walk out of the stadium halfway through the game, and say, "Forget this! You're all a bunch of losers." No, he waits and waits and encourages them and patiently works with them. Then he watches as they pull from behind. He doesn't quit on them.

Yet we're so quick to quit on God. We quote one verse, wait fifteen minutes, and if nothing seems to happen, we give up. Sometimes we're willing to wait twenty-four hours and then we're back knocking at God's door, "Hey God! What's the matter? What's taking so long to answer this prayer? I quoted Your Word just yesterday and nothing's happened yet. How come, God?"

Remember, the trying of your faith worketh patience. What do you do when you've prayed and nothing seems to be happening? You stand. And you keep standing for as long as it takes. That's faith.

While you're standing, you don't grit your teeth either. You rejoice and count it all joy because you know that even though you may not be able to see anything happening right before your eyes, God is working on your behalf. You continue to be patient, trusting God and His Word because you know that He is not a man that He should lie. He knows the *perfect timing* far better than we do.

God's Perfect Timing

Have you ever watched a car race or a track meet? In a long-distance race, you'll hear the announcer explain, "They're just holding back waiting; they're pacing themselves. They're not ready to pull out yet and sprint."

The young rookie runners or race car drivers get out and charge to the front immediately. They've got all kinds of energy to begin with, but it doesn't last. After a while, they either burn out physically or they burn out their tires and engines.

That never happens to the experienced racers though. Those old pros just sit back watching all the rookies burn out. They patiently wait, seemingly plodding along behind. But when the race gets down to the last few laps, they still have plenty of energy left. Then they begin to slowly make their way to the front. Eventually, they leave the rest of the pack behind in the dust, while they zip on to the finish line with the roar of the crowd in their ears.

I know these things because I used to run sprints. Sprinters cannot keep up with long-distance runners. Those long-distance runners are in a different class from sprinters. Sometimes when we were working out, our coach would make the sprinters run with the long-distance runners. Those guys could run and run and run and never get tired. Or so it seemed. They may not have been able to run as fast as the sprinters, but they knew what it meant to endure and last.

Whenever I'd have to run with those guys, I'd get so impatient. I'd try to pace myself to them, and the whole time I'd be thinking, *This is too slow; just way too slow.* So I'd burst on ahead. After a few laps I'd be burned out and they'd still be plodding along. I finally learned to settle down and be patient. When I'd pace myself to those long-distance guys, I found I could run longer too.

Life is not a forty-yard dash. We're in this race for the long run. Patience will help you stay in the race until the finish line: "... *press toward the mark for the prize of the high calling of God in Christ Jesus*" (Phil. 3:14). *"Know ye not that they which run in a race run all, but one receiveth the prize? So run, that ye may obtain"* (1 Cor. 9:24).

We won't ever obtain the prize if we don't endure. And that endurance comes from being disciplined. Those runners who run the marathons don't just get up one morning and decide, "Well, today I think it'd be fun to run the Boston Marathon."

They don't even get that far unless they've qualified

first in several other races. They just don't go out there and run twenty-six miles because they think it would be a fun thing to do. No, they are out there every day disciplining their bodies. Endurance, patience, and discipline is a part of them. That's how they then can go out and run and run and run until the finish line.

You may remember what happened a few years ago when a person tried to win an internationally televised marathon race by sneaking in at the end. This person came running across the finish line amid cheers and pandemonium. All the awards and acclaim went to him. Then someone noticed that he wasn't even sweating or breathing hard. In fact, they discovered that he hadn't even gotten into the race until the last mile or so. The award was then stripped from him. The man was totally humiliated in front of the whole world.

When he was interviewed, he said, "I just wanted to see what it felt like to be a winner." Listen, Jesus Christ has already made every believer a winner! At the end of this race called life there is a glorious prize waiting for us. But we won't ever make it to the finish line without patience.

Some people are looking for rewards before they're ready for them. In fact, this is one of the biggest roadblocks to a person's receiving from God. They jump on out there in faith believing God for things before they're ready, and before they have any knowledge of what they're going to face. Before they have the Word of God in them concerning the matter, they jump out and try to believe God for hundreds of dollars before they've ever believed Him for as much as two dollars.

David never faced the giant until he gained experience with the lion and bear first. David had total confidence he could face the giant because God had been with him when he faced the lion and the bear (1 Sam. 17:34-37).

I meet so many people who are trying to be where my Dad is — to walk in the kind of faith he has. But he has been at this for years. He didn't become successful overnight and neither will you.

You know, it wasn't until the fifties that my Dad realized we could believe God for finances. He'd known about healing, and we were walking in that knowledge. We knew how to believe God for healing, but we didn't know a thing about financial prosperity. Then Dad began to see in God's Word that he could also believe Him for finances. We finally saw in God's Word that we didn't have to be struggling all the time.

So we began to walk in faith concerning our finances. We began to believe God for financial prosperity. And God has blessed us. Oh, we went through some hard times in the process. You always do. But if you're spiritually mature, you can endure those hard knocks — the hard places.

Don't Ever Quit

You know what you do when those hard knocks hit? You keep standing steadfastly upon God's Word, refusing to quit. That's right. You may not enjoy watching boxing but there's something every good boxer knows. You don't ever quit. Boxer A may hit Boxer B with everything he's got, but Boxer B will win the fight every time if he just keeps punching back. Because Boxer A realizes, *I'm in trouble with this guy. I've just given him my best shot, and he's coming back with more punches. This guy intends to win no matter what.*

It's called endurance, patience, and stability. Stability is another word for patience. One of the main characteristics that any personnel department looks for when hiring a person is stability. They look at that person's past work record to see just how stable they are. Why? Because they know that stability affects every area of life. It affects how a person goes about accomplishing a job too. Stability affects the quality of your work.

An unstable, impatient person is always jumping around from one job to another. They get into first one thing and then another, this scheme and the next but they never find real success because they aren't willing to stay put when they hit a hard spot. You never grow that way. You'll never find success by quitting when hard times come — whether in the natural realm or in spiritual matters.

Let's take a person who wants to be a plumber. Let's say he has a dream of owning his own plumbing business one day. He knows plumbers make good money, and he decides that's what he wants to do with his life.

Guess where he starts? At the top? No. He starts out at the bottom, in the muck and mire. A plumber's helper knows what it means to endure hard places. Sometimes plumber's helpers have to crawl under houses where it's been leaking, and it's muddy, smelly, dirty, and hot. There is no ventilation, and besides all that, there are all kinds of bugs and rodents running around underneath that house with them.

Suppose that on the first day on the job, the plumber's helper says, "Forget this! I don't want to get dirty down there." By quitting he will never fulfill his dream of having that successful plumbing business. But if he hangs in there — if he's patient and learns the ropes — he will get promoted.

Patience will always promote you. Someone once said, "To know how to wait is the great secret of success." Someone else, when asked the secret of his success, said, "I stayed."

Haven't you ever noticed that the fruit worth waiting for is always the fruit that ripens slowest? You have to be patient and wait for it.

Patience always brings rewards for the godly: *"And let us not be weary in well doing: for in due season we shall reap, if we faint not"* (Gal. 6:9).

Patience develops strength of character. The sooner we form the habit of reacting patiently (rather than *impatiently*) to life's surprises, the easier our walk of faith will be through this earthly life.

We need to be patient with God, with ourselves, and with others. Patience is the ability to keep on keeping on, no matter what the circumstances are.

Paul praised the Church of Thessalonica with these words: *". . . we ourselves glory in you in the churches of God for your patience and faith in all your persecutions and tribulations that ye endure"* (2 Thess. 1:4).

At the time this was written, the Church knew what it meant to endure real persecution and tribulation. We don't face anything like what they faced, but as long as we are on this earth we are going to encounter things we must endure. We can do it with patience added to our faith.

". . . we count them happy which endure . . ." (James 5:11).

Chapter 6

Adding Godliness: Brotherly Kindness and Charity

And to knowledge temperance; and to temperance patience; and to patience godliness;
And to godliness brotherly kindness; and to brotherly kindness charity.

— 2 Peter 1:6,7

The next three character qualities Peter exhorts us to add to our faith are godliness, brotherly kindness, and charity. These three are so closely interwoven, you can hardly disconnect them.

Let's look at godliness first. Notice that the "g" in godliness is a small "g." It's not a capital "G." Developing godliness is something *we* have to do; God is not going to do it for us. God doesn't need to develop godliness; He already has it.

Godliness simply means possessing God-like attributes. We're the ones who have to develop godliness in our lives. Before we're saved, we don't have any godliness in us. As spiritual babes, we don't walk in a lot of godliness, but as we grow up spiritually, godliness should also grow in us. We don't stay spiritual babies.

At RHEMA Bible Church, baby dedications are a regular occurrence. It's funny to listen to parents' comments about their babies. The baby may only be a month old, but the parents have already decided he looks just like Grandpa. Or you'll hear them say, "Oh, look! He has John's nose, Mary's eyes, Bob's smile, and Ann's chin."

It's true! Children take on the attributes of their family members. The characteristics of parents can be seen in their children. If a child doesn't look like either of his parents, people joke, "I wonder where he came from?" We automatically expect a child to look something like his parents.

Certain traits are just part of your family heritage. One trait that runs in the "Hagin" family is that we're all strong-willed and strong-headed. We don't know what the word "quit" means. Every one of us Hagins is like that.

It's characteristic of our family heritage. And you have certain characteristics that everyone else in your family also has. Maybe your family members have big ears, or a small chin, or something else like that. But it's something that everyone who is part of your family seems to have. You just expect it. Whenever a new baby is born into the family, you look for those certain characteristics.

As children of God, we should also have the characteristics of our Heavenly Father. We should be just like our Father since we're part of His family. Godliness is simply being like God. His divine nature becomes a part of us because we're His children, and the attributes God has should also be active in our lives.

I think all Christians desire deep in their heart to be

godly. We want to do those things that are pleasing in God's sight. When we follow His ways, there's joy and peace. When we allow godliness to possess us, when we are yielded to God's will, following His paths, we can live a godly life with a clear conscience.

Godliness is conforming our mind and will to God's mind and will. True faith and a godly life cannot be separated from one another any more than a foundation can be separated from a building; a root can be separated from a tree trunk; or heat can be separated from a fire. They are inseparable. Faith and godliness are inseparable, or at least they should be. Someone with true faith will be godly; that's all there is to it.

We call ourselves Christians. That means we are to be like Christ. Sometimes we'd be wise to take an inventory and see just how much like Christ we really are. Carrying His Name is not a light thing. If we carry His Name, we should also carry His characteristics, His attributes, His traits, and be like Him. It should show; it should be obvious to those around us.

Godly Influence

There are plenty of examples in the Bible of people who lived truly godly lives. Godly lives enrich and influence everyone around them. For example, the king of Babylon couldn't stand Daniel's religion, but he couldn't rule his many provinces without Daniel's help either. So he let Daniel keep his God. Daniel was a living testimony in Babylon, a land of gross darkness, to the true and living God. Many others came to know the truth about God through Daniel. He lived a truly godly life and his impact was felt by all.

The king of Egypt wasn't thrilled with Joseph's religion either, but he knew he couldn't get Joseph's expert financial help and management skills without getting Joseph's godliness too. The two were inseparable. The king put up with Joseph's godliness to get his skills and abilities. As a result, Joseph saved his entire race.

The Bible says that Herod feared John the Baptist and protected him, knowing him to be a righteous and holy man. When Herod heard John, he was greatly puzzled; yet he liked to listen to him (Mark 6:20). John's godliness was a mystery to Herod yet it also was attractive to him. It impressed him so much that he didn't want to have John executed at all. The only reason John was beheaded was that Herod was tricked by his devious wife into having it done.

What did these three men — Daniel, Joseph, and John — all have in common? There was something about them that others could see. There was something about them that made them stand out in a crowd. They were different from everyone else. What was the difference? *Godliness.*

People can walk around saying they're Christians, but if their lives don't measure up, everyone knows it. Where the rubber meets the road is this: Are you truly living a godly life?

A godly life only comes one way. It only comes from a close relationship with God. Plenty of people claim to know God but they don't act anything like Him. It makes you wonder at times just how well they really know Him.

How much you really walk in godliness shows when the pressure is on. Remember the testimony of the seven sons of Sceva? They were going out trying to do things in the Name of the Lord. One day they tried to cast an evil spirit out of someone, and the evil spirit said, "... *Jesus I know, and Paul I know; but who are ye?"* (Acts 19:15).

They had no relationship with Jesus. They weren't godly at all. There was no godliness in them. And it showed! The sons of Sceva didn't have any authority to be doing what they were doing.

This is exactly why things don't seem to work out for some people. They go around with the appearance of godliness, making all the right faith confessions, but they're living ungodly lives. Then they wonder why things aren't working for them.

Doing His Will

Jesus Himself said:

MATTHEW 7:21-23
21 Not every one that saith unto me, Lord, Lord, shall enter into the kingdom of heaven; but he that doeth the will of my Father which is in heaven.
22 Many will say to me in that day, Lord, Lord, have we not prophesied in thy name? and in thy name have cast out devils? and in thy name done many wonderful works?

**23 And then will I profess unto them, I never
knew you: depart from me, ye that work iniquity.**

This passage sounds like Jesus was being harsh, but
He was really being honest. He definitely called things
like they were. Godliness is either a part of us or it's
not. We may be able to fool people, but there's no way
we can fool God! You just can't deceive Him!

It's time we made godliness a priority in our lives. As
we live godly lives, others around us will be affected
and changed by our example. Jesus set the standard for
godliness when He said *He could only do what he saw
his Father doing* (John 5:19).

If that becomes our attitude, our faith will work. Our
faith will be strong because our motives will be right,
and we'll be living a godly life to prove it.

You see, the life of Jesus must be lived and demon-
strated in our lives. We read the verses that say Christ
in us is the hope of glory; Christ in us is greater than he
who is in the world; Christ in us knows no defeat! But if
Christ truly lives in us, our lives will be godly. Godliness will be an outstanding trait of our lives.

You may have heard the story about the little boy
who was in the street with a bag full of fruit. He
dropped the fruit, and it rolled in every direction. No
one stopped to help him as he scurried about on the
sidewalk picking it all up. Everyone was much too busy
rushing to and from work to take notice of him or to
lend a hand.

So he just ran around dodging between their feet

trying to pick up all of his fruit. Some of the people hurrying by got angry at him and told him to get out of the way. Others shoved right past him, knocking him over. Then suddenly one man bent down to the little boy's level, gently touched him on the shoulder, looked him in the eye, and said, "Sonny, how can I help?" The boy's face lit up and they both bent down together and picked up the rest of the fruit. As the man was turning to go on his way, the boy tugged at his coat and looking up at him, asked, "Mister, are you God?"

That little boy saw something of God in that man. When people look at us, do they see God? Do we reflect Him to this world? Godliness is a daily thing! It's usually not very dramatic. It often goes unnoticed — unnoticed by others, that is, but it never goes unnoticed by God.

Godliness shows when no one else is around. What are you like when no one else is looking? Are you godly when you're alone? That's true godliness!

We need to develop godliness in our lives whether we ever get recognition for it or not. Godliness is being like God in the good times and in the hard times.

Compassion, Forgiveness, and Brotherly Kindness

What are some of God's attributes or characteristics that we should add to our faith to become godly? When I think of godliness or having a God-like character, one of the first things that comes to mind is compassion and forgiveness. God has a forgiving nature. He's more forgiving than any of us have ever been. Jesus told us to forgive and to never stop forgiving. We need to be a forgiving people and reach out to others with compassion like God does.

We need to quit being so hard on people and do what Paul said to do: *"Rejoice with them that do rejoice, and weep with them that weep"* (Rom. 12:15).

Compassion is not something that comes easily to us. That's why we're told to put on a heart of compassion. It's something we have to put on; something that takes effort.

This is where brotherly kindness comes into play. Brotherly kindness is godliness in action. Brotherly kindness means preferring your brother over yourself. It's being excited rather than getting jealous when you see your brother being blessed.

Kindness doesn't just flow out of our lives effortlessly. It has to be worked at, nourished, and encouraged. It takes effort to be kind to people because it often means going out of our way to be nice when it would be easier not to be nice.

The Bible is full of stories about those who showed forth brotherly kindness. One of the best examples is found in the life of Ruth. Ruth was a young Moabite widow when her mother-in-law, Naomi, decided to return to her homeland of Bethlehem. Ruth chose to go with her mother-in-law.

That was a great act of kindness on Ruth's part, because Ruth wasn't from the area of Bethlehem at all.

If she went to Bethlehem, it meant she'd probably never be married because she didn't belong to the Jewish race; Ruth was a Moabite. But she chose to go and help her mother-in-law rather than go back to her own home and family and find a husband there. She was being kind and compassionate, and it meant going out of her way to do so. But kindness always pays. In a very short time, Ruth's kindness was noticed by Boaz, a very wealthy man. Soon she became his wife! Ruth's kindness was rewarded in a big way.

We also have the story about the little widow lady who was kind to one of God's prophets, Elijah. Elijah had been sitting by a brook at God's command, depending on the ravens to feed him. God had also said that Elijah was to drink from the brook (1 Kings 17:4). But then the brook dried up! So God instructed Elijah to go to a widow in Zarephath (1 Kings 17:8,9).

Now when Elijah got there, he approached the widow and asked for some water to drink and some bread. This widow was not exactly thrilled to see Elijah, and she certainly wasn't overjoyed by his request. In fact, she answered him back, saying, "I don't have any bread. I have only a handful of flour in a jar and a little oil in a jug. And I'm gathering up these few sticks to build a fire and make a last meal for myself and my son, that we may eat it and then die" (1 Kings 17:12).

This widow was not in the best of spirits. Actually, she had already resigned herself to dying when this pushy stranger showed up wanting food and water! It was obviously not the best of times for her. And yet she did what Elijah requested. Not only did she and her son live, but sometime later when her son became sick and died, Elijah raised him from the dead! So her kindness paid off too.

It's easy to be kind to people in pleasant circumstances, but what about when the going is hard? Fair-weather kindness should have no place in a Christian's life. Godly kindness is permanent and enduring.

Godly kindness also goes the second mile. Remember Rebekah's act of kindness to Abraham's servant? When he asked for a drink, she volunteered to water his camels as well (Gen. 24:15-19). That was not a very pleasant job, I'm sure.

Rebekah's act of kindness had immediate consequences. First, she was given beautiful jewelry, and then she gained a rich husband from a wealthy family! Rebekah went the second mile and found out that kindness produces results.

We have all read the story of the Good Samaritan who showed kindness to someone who, because of his race, was supposed to be the Samaritan's enemy. Jesus' whole point in telling the story was to say, "Go and do the same."

Being a Good Samaritan simply means being willing to get involved in helping others — in going the second mile to minister to someone in need. That's why Jesus said:

MATTHEW 25:35-40,45
35 For I was an hungred, and ye gave me meat: I

was thirsty, and ye gave me drink: I was a
stranger, and ye took me in:
36 Naked, and ye clothed me: I was sick, and ye
visited me: I was in prison, and ye came unto me.
37 Then shall the righteous answer him, saying,
Lord, when saw we thee an hungred, and fed thee?
or thirsty, and gave thee drink?
38 When saw we thee a stranger, and took thee in?
or naked, and clothed thee?
39 Or when saw we thee sick, or in prison, and
came unto thee?
40 And the King shall answer and say unto them,
Verily I say unto you, Inasmuch as ye have done it
unto one of the least of these my brethren, ye have
done it unto me. . . .
45 Then shall he answer them, saying, Verily I say
unto you, Inasmuch as ye did it NOT to one of the
least of these, YE DID IT NOT to me.

Acts of kindness are evidence of a genuine relationship with the Lord. When we are kind to those in need,
we are actually showing kindness to Christ!

Sometimes you'll hear someone comment, "So-and-so
is a *real* Christian." Almost always, that expression
means the person is kind. People associate being kind
with being a true Christian. So does Jesus! To those
who are not kind, Jesus says, ". . . *Depart from me* . . ."
(Matt. 25:41).

Kindness is one of the three essentials the Lord
requires of man.

MICAH 6:8 *(Revised Standard Version)*
8 He has showed you, O man, what is good; and
what does the Lord require of you but to do

**justice, and TO LOVE KINDNESS, and to walk
humbly with your God.**

Zaccheus is an example of what brotherly kindness
can do in the life of an unbeliever. In his case, Zaccheus
was the recipient of the Lord's kindness (Luke 19:2-10).
When Jesus saw Zaccheus perched up in a tree, He
invited Himself to Zaccheus' house. That would have
been a great honor for anyone, but it was especially so
for Zaccheus because he was a tax collector. Tax collec-
tors at that time were not well liked by anyone. Everyone avoided Zaccheus, but Jesus reached out to him in
kindness. As a result, Zaccheus' life was totally trans-
formed by the undeserved kindness of Jesus.

If people would just be kind to others, it would go a
long way toward winning them to the Lord. It is the
kindness of God that leads men to repentance (Rom. 2:4
RSV).

We can also find in the Bible the story of Rahab's
kindness to the two spies sent to Jericho by the children
of Israel. Her life and the lives of her entire family were
spared due to her one act of simple and spontaneous
kindness. Jonathan's kindness to David led to his children's preservation after Jonathan had died. Elizabeth
kindly received Mary, the mother of Jesus, into her
home during Mary's pregnancy.

There are so many examples of kindness that we can
learn from in the Bible. Kindness should be one of our
highest aims along with walking in love. The last thing
Peter said we should add to our faith is charity. Another
word for Christian charity is love.

Christian Charity

Christian charity means love in action. If we'd make the decision to walk in love at all times, our faith would be as powerful as dynamite because faith worketh by love.

What is love? The best description we have of real love — real Christian charity — is found in the Bible.

1 CORINTHIANS 13:1-8
1   Though I speak with the tongues of men and of angels, and have not charity [love], I am become as sounding brass, or a tinkling cymbal.
2   And though I have the gift of prophecy, and understand all mysteries, and all knowledge; and though I have all faith, so that I could remove mountains, and have not charity [love], I am nothing.
3   And though I bestow all my goods to feed the poor, and though I give my body to be burned, and have not charity [love], it profiteth me nothing.
4   Charity [love] suffereth long, and is kind; charity [love] envieth not; charity [love] vaunteth not itself, is not puffed up,
5   Doth not behave itself unseemly, seeketh not her own, is not easily provoked, thinketh no evil;
6   Rejoiceth not in iniquity, but rejoiceth in the truth;
7   Beareth all things, believeth all things, hopeth all things, endureth all things.
8   Charity [love] never faileth. . . .

If you read through the above list carefully, you will see that love is described in terms of *actions*. Love is not just emotions and feelings. Scripture very clearly shows us that real charity — real love — is carried out in actions.

Only One Commandment

There is only one commandment given in the New Testament, and that commandment is to walk in love. You see, if we learn to walk in love at all times, we'll never break any of the other commandments that were given under the Law. If you love someone, you're not about to kill him, steal from him, or covet what is his.

If you have Christian love, you're going to love the unlovely too. I vividly remember preaching in a church one night, when two unsavory looking characters walked in and sat down on the back row. One of the guys had on a tank-top tee shirt with a picture of the devil on the front of it. On his shoulder there was a tattoo that said, "Born to raise hell." His jeans were so dirty, they probably would have stood in the corner by themselves. He had on sandals and his feet didn't look like they'd been washed in years. His hair was long and matted, and he smelled horrible. The other guy didn't look any better.

I noticed them the second they walked into the church. They stood out! I also noticed the reactions of people sitting near them. Some of those righteous saints of God turned around and looked at the two guys as if to say, "Who invited you? What are you doing here in our church?" If they'd had enough nerve to do so they probably would have said, "We don't allow your kind in here. Get out." They kept looking at these two guys out of the corners of their eyes, sort of pulling their righteous garments a little bit closer around them.

If it had been up to those church members, the two guys would have been escorted out by an usher. What kind of love is that? That night those two young men came forward during the altar call and got saved. They found out about the love of God but not with the help of anyone sitting by them.

Love is more than just talk. It's time to demonstrate our love to this world. You can talk all you want to about how much faith you've got, but I want to see your love in action. If you expect your faith to work, you have to demonstrate love.

> **JAMES 2:14-17** *(Living Bible)*
> **14 . . . what's the use of saying that you have faith and are Christians if you aren't proving it by helping others? Will that kind of faith save anyone?**
> **15 If you have a friend who is in need of food and clothing,**
> **16 and you say to him, "Well, good-bye and God bless you; stay warm and eat hearty," and then don't give him clothes or food, what good does that do?**
> **17 So you see, it isn't enough just to have faith. You must also do good to prove that you have it. Faith that doesn't show itself by good works is no faith at all — it is dead and useless.**

I'm tired of seeing the Body of Christ pulled and twisted and torn to pieces when it's not necessary. One of our RHEMA graduates tells the story about a young boy who died. This graduate got a knock on his door one day and the people wanted him to go over to someone's house because their little boy had just drowned in the swimming pool. When he got there, he realized he had a son the same age as the child who had drowned. He also realized it wasn't time to walk in there like he was "Super Faith Man" or something.

It was time to minister to this family at the point of their need in love. So he just walked in, put his arm around the father, told him he loved him and was there to stand with him. Those people didn't need a "big faith man" right then. They needed love. Later on he knew they would need encouragement in their faith to overcome such a disappointment. But that was certainly no time to say "Brother, where's your faith? Why are you crying?"

There are times when we need to put on the face of a lion and be bold, stern, and strong. Then there are other times when we need to be very soft, very tender, and caring. Love knows the difference. That's growing up spiritually.

Love Covers

Another thing we need to realize about love is that love covers a multitude of sins (1 Peter 4:8). What does that mean? It means we don't stomp all over someone if they blow it. It's so sad to see someone who's been hurt because they did something wrong and everyone turned on them. Instead of helping that person when he's down, most Christians want to kick him down further. The Church is the only army that shoots its own wounded! As soon as someone makes a mistake or is caught in some sin, everyone gets on the telephone and spreads the news all over the country. Is that love?

The Bible tells us that when we see a brother overtaken in a fault: ". . . *ye which are spiritual, restore such an one in the spirit of meekness; considering thyself, lest thou also be tempted"* (Gal. 6:1).

Do you throw your child out the door if he makes a mistake? Of course not. In fact, I know some families who have gone bankrupt trying to help their children out of trouble by hiring lawyers and doing everything they can to help them. Yet what do we as the family of God do when we see someone who's down? Instead of helping those who are in trouble, we circle like vultures waiting for them to go under! And we talk about them in the meantime. That's sad.

Instead of talking about someone and reminding everyone of their past sins, we need to reach out in love and restore them. Love covers. If we're spiritually mature, we'll overlook a person's inconsistencies and love them back into line. Instead of taking a step toward someone and ministering to them at the point of their need, we stand up on our high pedestal of faith, look down at them and blast them with the Word of God. "Why don't you have some faith? If you had any faith you wouldn't be down there. You'd be living like me." That's not love.

I heard a story about a young woman who was in the

hospital for emergency eye surgery. Without it she'd go blind. A man she had never met or seen before walked into her hospital room, and said, "Sister, you're in sin. If you weren't in sin you wouldn't be here in this hospital with this problem. Where's your faith? You need to repent and leave this hospital." This guy just heaped all kinds of guilt and condemnation on that woman and then left her in total confusion trying to figure out what she'd done wrong to deserve this eye problem. Then someone else walked in with the love of God, ministered to her, and she was totally healed!

Which of those people was walking in love? It's obvious. Love never fails. Loving God and loving people go together. You can't have one without the other.

If you really love God, you will love people. You will reach out in love to them and do what love does.

Faith worketh by love (Gal. 5:6). If we add love to our faith, it will work. Our faith will be powerful.

Chapter 7
The Mature Never Fall

Throughout this book, I have been talking about what we're supposed to add to our faith. We've looked at what's on the other side of "And." Besides all the blessings, besides being a partaker of the divine nature, Peter told us to add some things to our faith. He said, *"And beside this, . . ."* meaning besides all the blessings, what else is there?

Then Peter goes on to tell us that we're to diligently add to our faith such things as virtue, knowledge, temperance, patience, godliness, brotherly kindness, and charity.

Now, after reading this book, I hope you're convinced that it's a good idea to add these character qualities to your faith. But if for some reason you're not totally convinced yet, there's still one last reason to follow Peter's instructions. Peter completes this section of Second Peter chapter 1 with the following verses:

> **2 PETER 1:8-11**
> **8 For if these things be in you, and abound, they make you that ye shall neither be barren nor unfruitful in the knowledge of our Lord Jesus Christ.**
> **9 But he that lacketh these things is blind, and cannot see afar off, and hath forgotten that he was purged from his old sins.**
> **10 Wherefore the rather, brethren, give diligence**

**to make your calling and election sure: for if ye do
these things, ye shall never fall:
11 For so an entrance shall be ministered unto
you abundantly into the everlasting kingdom of
our Lord and Saviour Jesus Christ.**

Once we've added to our faith — virtue, knowledge,
temperance, patience, godliness, brotherly kindness
and charity — once we've worked on adding all these
things, what happens? We become fruitful in the knowledge of our Lord Jesus Christ, and the Scripture tells
us that we'll never fall — *never*. That also means without these character qualities operating in our lives, we
remain barren, unfruitful and it's easier for us to fall.

No one who calls himself a Christian would know-
ingly want to be unfruitful. Every Christian I know is
quick to say, "Oh, yes, I desire to be fruitful for my
Lord." That's the heart desire of every true Christian.
But, you see, there are some steps we have to take to be
fruitful. It doesn't just happen. It's not something that's
going to fall out of the sky on us. We make it happen by
adding to our faith all these things that Peter told us to
add.

The Bible tells us that we are to be perfect even as
Christ was perfect (Matt. 5:48). We are to strive for that
perfection. The quality of a man's life is in direct pro-
portion to his commitment to excellence or perfection.
Character is the most important determinant of a person's overall success. Only strength of character will
endure and last through thick and thin.

The way that we excel — the way we become more

perfect or mature — is to add these things that Peter talked about. As we do, our lives will mature and bear fruit. It's guaranteed. These qualities are supposed to be *in* us. All of Jesus' qualities are in us. The big question is, how much of Him are we letting out?

Look at the list again — virtue, knowledge, temperance, patience, godliness, brotherly kindness, and charity. Wouldn't you say that Jesus had all these qualities fully operational in His life? We can have them too. For as He is, so are we in this world (1 John 4:17).

Lasting Fruit

What does it mean to be fruitful? It means we are producing something of lasting value for the Kingdom of God. Do you realize that the only thing that's going to last is what we do for eternity? All the rest of it is going to burn one day. That's a sobering thought, isn't it? It would be a worthwhile thing if before doing anything we asked ourselves if that is what God wants. Only then will it be fruitful. You see, the arm of flesh can accomplish a lot, but in the end it won't last.

Only those things that are done in God's will can truly bear lasting fruit. Those things that are done with virtue, knowledge, temperance, patience, godliness, brotherly kindness, and charity will bear fruit that lasts.

These qualities are supposed to abound in us. *The Amplified Bible* says that they should *increasingly* abound! That means they keep growing and getting stronger and stronger. A spiritually mature person never stops growing.

A minister once made this statement: "If you're green, you're still growing; if you're ripe, you're starting to rot!" As Christians, we never stop growing. We should always continue to mature into the full stature of Christ. That should be our goal — to be more like Jesus every day. Tomorrow I should be more like Jesus than I am today. And the day after that, I should be even more like Him.

As we develop the character qualities that I have written about in this book, we will become more like Jesus. We will become more spiritually mature. We will be more fruitful in our knowledge of Him.

2 PETER 1:9
9   But he that lacketh these things is blind, and cannot see afar off, and hath forgotten that he was purged from his old sins.

Another way to say this is that some of us have become so spiritually shortsighted, we've forgotten that we've been forgiven of our old sins. This verse implies that if we've forgotten about our old sins, it's easy to neglect developing the qualities of a sin-free life. You see, if you're working on developing those things that Peter said to add to your faith, it's going to be very difficult for any sin to cling to you.

Having knowledge of these character qualities, walking in them, and applying them to our lives is what counts. These are the things that pertain to life and godliness! The more you exercise them; the more you develop them; the more they become part of you; then the more the life of God manifests in and through you. The "zoe" life of God in you will begin to flow out to others.

It's easy sometimes to forget where we've been. If we forget, then when we look at someone else who's struggling, it's easy to say, "Where's your faith, Brother? What's wrong with you?" We get critical and judgmental when we forget just what we've been forgiven of ourselves! Peter calls that blindness. We should never forget from whence we came. Remember, *But for the grace of God, there go I!* We need to walk in brotherly kindness, patience, and love toward another brother or sister who's having difficulties.

The Bible says that if we see a brother in sin, we're to meekly help him back up again. We're not to judge, criticize, and talk to everyone else about what horrible things he has done! Don't ever forget the forgiveness of Jesus you have received. Freely you have received, freely give.

I don't ever want to be accused of spiritual blindness. Blindness in the natural is an awful thing. It affects so many areas of your life. I have the utmost respect for blind people and how they manage their lives. But I would never want to be blind myself because I recognize the challenges a blind person faces. When we're spiritually blind, we risk running into all kinds of trouble. Fortunately, Peter showed us how to stay spiritually sighted with 20-20 vision.

If you'll always remember these qualities that Peter said to add to your faith and keep walking in them, you'll never go spiritually blind. Your spiritual eyesight will stay healthy and strong.

Never Means *Never*

2 PETER 1:10
10 Wherefore the rather, brethren, give diligence to make your calling and election sure: for if ye DO THESE THINGS, ye shall never fall.

If you strive to do these things in your life, you won't have any trouble with falling, you won't have any trouble with being overcome by temptation. If you do what things? Walk in virtue, knowledge, temperance, patience, godliness, brotherly kindness, and charity.

If we have these character qualities added to our faith and we're walking in them, temptation has nothing with which to trip us and ensnare us. The Bible says with these things active in our lives, we shall *never fall*!

That's quite a promise. Especially in these days when everywhere we look we seem to see ministers and Christians falling into one sin or another. I'm not trying to pass judgment on these dear brothers and sisters in the Lord. But somewhere along the line, they failed to add those things Peter said to add to their faith. For if they had, they would never have fallen.

God's word is true. He is not a man that He should lie. And His Word doesn't ever lie either. It means exactly what it says. If it says we shall *never fall*, then that means we shall never fall. It is entirely possible for a Christian to live a life without ever falling! We should all strive for that level of spiritual maturity. But, it takes work.

Notice, once again, Peter says give diligence to making your calling and election sure. There's that word again — diligence! Remember, we started by saying that diligence is the key to it all. You have to be diligent in adding all these wonderful qualities to your life. They don't just fall on you. As you are diligent to do it, then you become fruitful and mature spiritually.

You know, one of the things that amazes me the most about this particular passage we've been studying here in Second Peter is that *Peter* wrote it. I find that very amusing or ironic because it was Peter who publicly denied Jesus, remember? He didn't do it just once, either, but three times. He had the opportunity to make it right after the first mistake, but he didn't. Peter knew what it meant to fall.

He had failed Jesus miserably. He knew it, and what's worse he knew that Jesus knew it. If anyone had reason to feel like a total failure, it was Peter. Yet he went on to discover how to keep from falling. He told us how to *never fall*.

When Peter was walking with Jesus, he never did grow up spiritually. He was always doing or saying rash things. Peter may have been the inspiration for that phrase: "He's always putting his foot in his mouth."

It took a catastrophe in his life to turn him around.

Somewhere after the time he ran from Jesus, pretending that he never knew Him, and before the time he wrote Second Peter, the man Peter changed drastically! Peter got hold of what it meant to grow up spiritually. And he grew up.

When Peter stood in the courtroom during Jesus' trial, he said he never knew Him. But later when he was accused of being a disciple of Jesus, he stood up boldly and declared the gospel — so boldly and courageously in fact that the people were astonished. They looked at him and said, "How is it that this ignorant and unlearned man can speak like he's speaking? How can he do the things he's doing?" The Bible says the skeptics knew that Peter had been with Jesus! That's the only explanation they had. Peter had become like Jesus! And they couldn't argue with that!

Heaven's Ambassadors

When we grow up spiritually and develop some of these qualities Peter exhorts us to have in our lives, people are going to look at us, and say, "That person has been with Jesus. That person knows Jesus. He acts just like Him." They'll see Jesus in your actions, your words, and your deeds.

As we do what Peter exhorted us to do, we will grow up. Peter did — there's no doubt about that. I think Peter's a good teacher and example for us. If it worked in his life — someone who was a failure in many ways — it will work in our lives too.

We are Jesus' representatives on this earth. The Bible calls us ambassadors (2 Cor. 5:20). One thing about ambassadors in the natural — they know how to act. They don't do anything to bring a bad name on the country they're representing. If they do, they're removed from their position quickly.

We are ambassadors for the King of Kings, for the highest kingdom there is. We represent the best there is. We are citizens of that heavenly Kingdom. It's time we started acting like it, don't you think? It's time for the Church to grow up.

We can be the ambassadors He's called us to be. As we add to our faith, we will see our lives changed and the lives of people around us changed more and more into the likeness of Him. I like what John said, "I must decrease; He must increase" (John 3:30). Our goal should be that Jesus increase in us daily — that more and more of Him be seen in our lives each day.

Do you want to grow up spiritually? Start adding to your faith today. With all diligence, add to your faith — virtue, knowledge, temperance, patience, godliness, brotherly kindness, and charity.

We are facing the last days. Only those who have learned how to be spiritually mature will endure to the end. They will not fall. The rest will fall by the wayside. You have to make the choice which way you will go — the way of standing or the way of falling! You can only go one way or the other. It's all determined by your spiritual maturity.

God is looking for those who are not affected by the

circumstances of life. He needs people who can shout when the sky is black. He needs people who are stead-fast, those who can endure when the storm is howling all around them and it looks like there's no way out. He needs those who can still whistle and sing, "Standing on the promises that cannot fail, when the howling storms of doubt and fear assail. Standing on the promises I shall prevail!"

That's the kind of people God is looking for in this last hour of the Church. Those are the people He can use — spiritually mature people!

It's a hard thing to grow up sometimes, because with growth comes responsibility. If you're going to be strong spiritually; if you're going to develop Christ-like atti-tudes and a Christ-like spirit; if you're going to have the characteristics of God; then you need to get on the other side of *"And beside this. . . ."*

Unless you begin to spiritually mature, you're going to find yourself in a world of hurt in the days to come. Being spiritually mature is not running around making a bunch of faith confessions and living a defeated, ungodly life. Being spiritually mature is not always looking for some new, deep revelation. Real spiritual maturity is walking in virtue, knowledge, temperance, patience, godliness, brotherly kindness, and charity.

Eat a Healthy Diet

I know this book has not been a light, easy book to read. I wrote it with the sincere desire to help you. I pray that it will help bring correction to areas of your life that need correction, and that it will exhort you to become more and more like Christ every day. If we'll take to heart what Peter told us, we will grow spiritually and be healthy and strong in the Lord.

I challenge you in this book to get on the other side of "And." *"And beside this, . . . add to your faith . . ."* (2 Peter 1:5). Besides all the blessings, add to your faith what Peter said to add, and you will not fall.

We so often hear teaching and read books on prosperity, healing, faith, and all those wonderful Bible subjects. But that's just part of the package. It's what I call the dessert; it's the good part. Prosperity, healing, and faith are the icing on the cake. But it's these other qualities — virtue, knowledge, temperance, patience, godliness, brotherly kindness, and charity — that will make you strong.

It's spinach, peas, carrots, and meat that build strong bodies, not desserts. Sure, it's fun to eat cake and ice-cream, but a steady diet of that will leave you weak and sickly. You'll never grow healthy in your body on that kind of diet.

Yet we have a lot of people who want all the "cake" and "ice-cream" parts of the gospel — the healing, prosperity, and faith — but they don't want to eat what will make them healthy and strong spiritually.

There's a lot more to this Christian life we're living than just prosperity, faith, and healing. This really began to dawn on me as I traveled overseas. I began to see the lost as I had never seen them before. It makes you get down on your knees and begin to search your heart, and ask, "God, am I being selfish? Help me to mature so I can take the whole gospel, not just a part of it, to the whole world. People need it all."

We need it all, too, amen? It's not just the exciting parts of the gospel that we are to incorporate into our lives; we need to also incorporate the nitty-gritty, down-to-earth, practical things that will cause us to grow. These are the things that Peter exhorted us to add to our faith. When we do, we will accomplish great things for God's glory and honor in this earth.

Press on to the high calling that is yours in Christ Jesus.